'I have just spent some time re  the Lord is going to use it. something written by a friend ' the walk that is spoken about i centred book that is great to use in you hope you will not only read it but get copies to give to others.'
George Verwer DD, founder and former International Director of OM

'Clive is a true pioneer. His quiet witness over many years has impacted countless lives. He's the sort of humble practitioner from whom I love to learn.'
Pete Greig, 24-7 Prayer; Emmaus Road

'A great book – there is a clarity and challenge to live with the real goal in full focus. I certainly feel encouraged to continue pressing on for that reward of greater closeness to Christ after reading it.'
Sanjay Rajo, leader of Naujavan Asian Christian youth movement

'I have been greatly blessed reading this book. It reads like worship and is thoroughly biblical in dealing with a subject that has been neglected for many years.'
John Symons, retired missionary and pastor

'Clive Thorne has an extraordinary ability to make complex things simple and accessible to his readers, and this book does just that. It is a stimulating challenge to ensure that we maintain a healthy marriage of belief and behaviour in the outworking of our Christian faith. A great read!'
Simon Orton, pastor Kings Church, Southampton

HIDDEN IN PLAIN SIGHT

Discovering heaven's treasure

Clive Thorne

instant
apostle

First published in Great Britain in 2017

Instant Apostle
The Barn
1 Watford House Lane
Watford
Herts
WD17 1BJ

Copyright © Clive Thorne 2017

All rights reserved. No portion of this book may be reproduced or transmitted in any form or by any means, electronic or mechanical, including photocopying, recording, or by any information storage and retrieval system, without permission in writing from the publisher.

Unless otherwise indicated, all Scripture quotations are taken from the Holy Bible, New International Version® Anglicized, NIV® Copyright © 1979, 1984, 2011 by Biblica, Inc.® Used by permission. All rights reserved worldwide.

Scripture references marked 'AMP' are taken from the Amplified® Bible (AMP), copyright © 2015 by The Lockman Foundation. Used by permission. www.Lockman.org.

Scripture references marked 'NKJV are taken from the New King James Version®. Copyright © 1982 by Thomas Nelson. Used by permission. All rights reserved.

Scripture references marked 'NLT' are taken from the Holy Bible, New Living Translation, copyright ©1996, 2004, 2007 by Tyndale House Foundation. Used by permission of Tyndale House Publishers, Inc., Carol Stream, Illinois 60188. All rights reserved.

Every effort has been made to seek permission to use copyright material reproduced in this book. The publisher apologises for those cases where permission might not have been sought and, if notified, will formally seek permission at the earliest opportunity.

The views and opinions expressed in this work are those of the author and do not necessarily reflect the views and opinions of the publisher.

British Library Cataloguing-in-Publication Data

A catalogue record for this book is available from the British Library

This book and all other Instant Apostle books are available from Instant Apostle:

Website: www.instantapostle.com

E-mail: info@instantapostle.com

ISBN 978-1-909728-64-6

Printed in Great Britain

For more information please contact:
Clive Thorne
Southampton Lighthouse International Church
St Mary's Rd
Southampton, UK
SO14 0BB
Website: www.lighthouseicc.org.uk

The kingdom of heaven is like treasure hidden in a field. When a man found it, he hid it again, and then in his joy went and sold all he had and bought that field.
(Matthew 13:44)

For those whose eyes see and ears hear.

Contents

Acknowledgements

With many thanks to the editor Sheila Jacobs, and also to Simon Orton, Manoj Raithatha, Kuldip Rajo and John Symons for their helpful reviews and suggestions.

1
Why This Book?

The night that I first heard the gospel, I knew that I had found a treasure beyond compare. This was the good news that God had become a man, lived a perfect life healing all who came to him, doing miracle after miracle and uttering words of such amazing love, wisdom and goodness, and then died a horrific death to save me from my sins. If God existed and loved me, then there was no greater way to show that love than for him to become a man and for that man to die for me.

I was a messed-up, depressive youngster who had been searching for the meaning of a life that seemed otherwise pointless. The prospect of a real moment-by-moment relationship with a God who loved me so much overwhelmed my heart. I went straight home to my college room and prayed to ask God's forgiveness for my sins and offer my life to follow him. The whole room was suddenly full of someone I could not see coming towards me as I was lying in bed. It felt like I was sick and this was like a nurse coming to make me well, and that presence went into me very peacefully and I fell asleep. From that moment everything in my life changed. I had found the most precious thing in all the universe – a relationship with the God who made us and loves us even to death on a cross.

God suddenly became real in my life and was responding to my prayers. It was as if before I had been in a darkened room searching for someone, and then the light came on and a pair of hands gently turned my shoulders to see him. The whole world looked different too! The attraction of a career as an Oxford-trained scientist faded to insignificance beside the wonder of following Jesus wherever he would lead me. I was ready to give everything up there and then, but as I prayed, it seemed right to at least finish the degree I had started.

During the remaining years at college, I gave serious time to studying the Bible, learning all I could about the Christian life from older believers and spending much time in prayer seeking God's specific will for my future. I graduated in July 1978 and was in India with the mission Operation Mobilisation by November. All I have ever wanted to do since is to serve him and tell everyone I possibly can about his love and good news.

Moving from the dreaming towers and spires of Oxford to sleeping on the floor, washing from a bucket and being without books, radio or television (mobile phones and the internet were not yet invented!) in India was not easy. Add to that a boiling climate (from about 28°C in the winter to as much as 55°C in the summer), scorching food, stomach trouble on and off for the first six months because of the water, and a culture so different from my own that it was hard to relate to the extremely friendly Indians. It turned out to be one of the hardest periods of my life, but God was with me through it all, and I was learning about myself and changing. No matter what I went through, he always remained my treasure and the rock that supported me, as he has until this day.

The Bible says that the kingdom of God is like a hidden treasure: 'The kingdom of heaven is like treasure hidden in a field. When a man found it, he hid it again, and then in his joy went and sold all he had and bought that field' (Matthew 13:44). In fact, the idea of treasure, reward or inheritance in heaven is scattered throughout the Old and New Testaments, but so often seemingly unknown or overlooked by those of us who trust that by God's grace we are going to spend eternity there. This passage in Matthew is claiming that this treasure is so wonderful that the person who finds it will sell all they have to obtain it. *And sell everything with joy!*

Is that how you see salvation, a relationship with God? We can find it hard enough to commit to attending church regularly, spending daily time in prayer or reading the Bible, let alone selling everything with joy.

If we don't see our relationship with God as worth that much, then something is badly wrong with our idea about what is involved in following Jesus. Listen to the apostle Paul: 'I consider everything a loss compared to the surpassing greatness of knowing Christ Jesus my Lord, for whose sake I have lost all things. I consider them rubbish, that I may gain Christ' (Philippians 3:8, NIV 1984). He goes on to say that the all-consuming priority in his life is to know Christ and to press on to win the prize in heaven for which God called him.[1]

---

[1] Philippians 3:10–14.

Do we live like this if we have come to know Jesus? Or are we distracted still by the things of this world? Do we ultimately value money, career, pleasure, family, wife, husband, parents or children more than knowing God? This book is written to examine this treasure or prize in heaven and to find out why we so often fail to see its worth, and what we can do to obtain it.

Inheritance

The idea that God has an inheritance planned for his people is found throughout the Bible from beginning to end, and goes all the way back to God calling Abraham to leave his homeland and extended family and travel to another country which his descendants would inherit. Abraham left everything and followed God's call by faith because he considered whatever God was promising to be worth leaving everything else behind to obtain. 'By faith Abraham, when called to go to a place he would later receive as his inheritance, obeyed and went, even though he did not know where he was going. By faith he made his home in the promised land like a stranger in a foreign country; he lived in tents, as did Isaac and Jacob, who were heirs with him of the same promise. For he was looking forward to the city with foundations, whose architect and builder is God' (Hebrews 11:8–10, NIV 1984).

Abraham, of course, never did own any of the promised land, except the place where he was buried. This passage and verse 16 tell us that he was trusting God for a heavenly inheritance, not one in this world. We are called to leave our attachment to everything else to obtain the treasure/inheritance of the kingdom of heaven: 'In the same way, those of you who do not give up everything you have cannot be my disciples' (Luke 14:33).

This idea of inheritance is carried on hundreds of years later in the time of Moses when God promises to rescue the Israelites from slavery in Egypt to bring them to inherit the land he promised to their ancestors Abraham, Isaac and Jacob. The whole story of the exodus from Egypt and journey to the promised land is a picture of the Christian life as we journey to our promised land of heaven.

The Israelites were born into slavery in Egypt and we are born into slavery to our sinful human nature.[2] They were saved out of slavery by trusting in the blood of a perfect male lamb being spread on their doorposts at Passover so that the judgement would pass over them.[3] We are saved by the blood of the perfect Lamb of God,[4] Jesus (who died on the day of preparation for the Passover feast around 1,400 years later), being applied by faith to us so that the judgement of our sins passes over us.

They then passed through the sea to escape Egypt, and we pass through the waters of baptism. They journeyed through a desert sustained by water from a rock and fed by manna from heaven,[5] and we journey through the dry and weary land of this world sustained by the supernatural life of Jesus who said, in John 4:14, 'whoever

---

[2] John 8:34.

[3] Exodus 12:1–13.

[4] 1 Corinthians 5:7.

[5] 1 Corinthians 10:1–6.

drinks the water I give them will never thirst. Indeed, the water I give them will become in them a spring of water welling up to eternal life', and in John 6:51, 'I am the living bread that came down from heaven. Whoever eats this bread will live for ever.'

They received God's laws written on stone tablets; we receive God's law written on our hearts as the Holy Spirit convicts our conscience.[6] They were headed to a land in which God had prepared an inheritance for them; we are heading towards such an inheritance prepared for us in heaven: 'Come, you who are blessed by my Father; take your inheritance, the kingdom prepared for you since the creation of the world' (Matthew 25:34).[7] They had to fight battles to displace the people already inhabiting the land;[8] we have to fight temptation and the spiritual forces of evil to change our behaviour and be transformed into the image of Jesus to gain our spiritual inheritance.

The original generation of Israelites who followed Moses out of Egypt did not, however, gain their inheritance in the promised land because they refused to trust God to defeat the enemies occupying the land. They remained God's people whom he fed with the manna and protected from attack, but they failed to receive the inheritance God had wanted to give them.[9]

We also need to heed that warning as reiterated to the first-century Christians in the region of Galatia in Galatians 5:19–21: 'The acts of the sinful nature are

---

[6] Jeremiah 31:31–33.

[7] See also 1 Peter 1:3–4.

[8] Deuteronomy 20:16–18.

[9] Numbers 14:20–23.

obvious: sexual immorality, impurity and debauchery; idolatry and witchcraft; hatred, discord, jealousy, fits of rage, selfish ambition, dissensions, factions and envy; drunkenness, orgies, and the like. I warn you, as I did before, that those who live like this will not inherit the kingdom of God', and 6:7–8, 'Do not be deceived: God cannot be mocked. A man reaps what he sows. The one who sows to please his sinful nature, from that nature will reap destruction; the one who sows to please the Spirit, from the Spirit will reap eternal life' (NIV 1984). This is not talking about losing our salvation, but rather losing the reward/inheritance we could be storing up in heaven by failing to live a life in the power of the Holy Spirit.

Treasure in heaven

We are commanded by Jesus in the New Testament to build treasure in heaven: 'Do not store up for yourselves treasures on earth, where moths and vermin destroy, and where thieves break in and steal. But store up for yourselves treasures in heaven, where moths and vermin do not destroy, and where thieves do not break in and steal' (Matthew 6:19–20). Jesus is contrasting all the things that we can chase after in this world, which are all temporary and will pass away, with things of eternal value that we can never lose. This is not an optional extra for super-Christians but a command to all of us for our own spiritual good.

Imagine someone was emigrating to another country and never going to return to their place of birth. Before they leave they want to throw a party and so they buy £10,000 worth of flowers and plants for their garden. When their friends arrive, they would be thinking, 'What on earth are these people doing, spending all this money on this garden which they are going to leave behind and never see again; surely they would be better off spending that money on their new house abroad?' It would be seen as a wasteful and extravagant use of money to make a spectacular show of something that they were leaving behind.

We, however, know of a certainty that we are one day going to die and leave behind all our physical goods and worldly achievements. As Christians, we believe that we are going to spend eternity in heaven. How foolish, then, to spend all our time and energy building up our life here, which will one day be dust and ashes, rather than building treasure in heaven which will be waiting for us and will last forever. It would indeed be wise to sell everything to buy that hidden treasure in the field. Jim Elliot, an American missionary who was killed whilst trying to bring the gospel message to an unreached tribe in the jungles of Ecuador, said, 'He is no fool who gives what he cannot keep to gain that which he cannot lose.'

There is nothing wrong in working hard to provide for ourselves and our families and to have something to be able to help those in need; nothing wrong in using the resources and wealth God has given us to serve his purposes. Rich and powerful people can use their money and influence to bring about much good. God can use rich and poor alike but if our career, acquiring wealth or any earthly pursuit becomes our main priority before loving and serving God, we will be missing out on treasure in heaven for short-term gain in this life.

It is not so much about physically giving everything away (although that may be involved) as where our heart and attachment are. Paul puts the way we should view these things like this: 'those who buy something, as if it were not theirs to keep; those who use the things of the world, as if not engrossed in them. For this world in its present form is passing away' (1 Corinthians 7:30–31).

If all this is true, then what kind of lives ought we to be living as we follow the Lord Jesus Christ? 'Command those who are rich in this present world not to be arrogant nor to put their hope in wealth, which is so uncertain, but to put their hope in God, who richly provides us with everything for our enjoyment. Command them to do good, to be rich in good deeds, and to be generous and willing to share. In this way they will lay up treasure for themselves as a firm foundation for the coming age, so that they may take hold of the life that is truly life' (1 Timothy 6:17–19).

But what exactly is that treasure?

2
Treasure Beyond Price

God said to Abram – before he had any children and his name was changed to Abraham, and before he owned any part of the promised land that his descendants would inherit – 'Do not be afraid, Abram. I am your shield, your very great reward' (Genesis 15:1).

A very great reward

In what way is God 'a very great reward'? God is the Creator of all things and the source of everything good. I was trained as a biologist and have always been impressed by the beauty of nature and this living world. I like long walks in the countryside and those wonderful wildlife programmes on the TV. Humanity has a long history of wonder and awe at the universe around us, often even worshipping aspects of the natural world, particularly the sun and moon and certain animals, but these are just objects that have been made by God the Creator.

Do you enjoy mountain scenery, the beauty of a flower, the glorious diversity of a rainforest or a coral reef – the visual impact of a myriad of colourful fish darting to and fro amongst the branches of coral – or the simple ever-changing beauty of the sky? Do we not marvel at the spectacle of the stars at night – 100 billion stars in our galaxy and more than 100 billion galaxies expanding outwards into the unimaginable distances of space? Or our own sun, where just one flame on its surface dwarfs the whole earth? What about the power of a thunderstorm, the austere beauty of a desert, the hidden depths of the ocean, or the wonder of every snowflake being different and unique? Whatever we might marvel at in the universe around us, God is better because he made it all.

Or do you appreciate the skill of humankind in producing soaring symphonies or energising music and dance, the inventiveness of fictional tales with the power to move our hearts, or the glories of the art world? What about the athletic achievements of sportsmen and women, or the excitement of a closely fought football match or tennis tournament? God is better because he made humanity with all our creativity in his image, and so everything we have achieved is simply a tiny reflection of our Creator.

What would an artist give to be friends with Monet or Michelangelo, a musician with Mozart or maybe Michael Jackson, a physicist with Isaac Newton or Einstein, or a writer with Shakespeare or Dickens? To know God is better, as he gave the power of artistic or scientific inspiration to them all!

Whatever is true, noble, right, pure, lovely, admirable, excellent or praiseworthy,[10] God is the source of it all and

---

[10] Philippinas 4:8.

better by far. If we had the ability to capture the fleeting beauty of a sunset in a fantastic piece of art, create a symphony that would move men to tears, write words that would change the course of history, or soar amongst the stars to explore and settle other earth-like planets, it would all be as nothing to knowing the One who made it all. How well do you know him? Do you want to know him more?

But God's power and creativity is just the beginning as we lift our eyes to see the light of his love and start to understand what true love really is and how much God loves us. King David had begun to grasp this love of God, as we see in Psalm 63:1–5: 'O God, you are my God, earnestly I seek you; my soul thirsts for you, my body longs for you, in a dry and weary land where there is no water. I have seen you in the sanctuary and beheld your power and your glory. Because your love is better than life, my lips will glorify you. I will praise you as long as I live, and in your name I will lift up my hands. My soul will be satisfied as with the richest of foods' (NIV 1984).

David is convinced that God's love is better than anything this life (which is described as 'a dry and weary land', as he was actually in a desert) could offer, and so he is desperately seeking God's presence and the comfort of his love. He has experienced God's presence before, and so has faith that God will draw near to him again and satisfy his longing. We were created in the image of God, who is love, to be in relationship with him, and we can never be fully satisfied with anything but the perfect love of God. Nothing else, no human love no matter how wonderful, will ultimately satisfy that deepest longing in the human soul.

God's love is better than a bride's happiness on her wedding day, better than a mother's joy at the birth of her child, better than a man winning his true love, better indeed than anything we could ever achieve. And not just a bit better – infinitely better, no comparison, an utterly different league! He is the source of all goodness, and made the power of thought and feeling we experience as love. How much have we really laid hold on this love? It was Paul's prayer for the church at Ephesus that they would grasp this more and more: 'I pray that you, being rooted and established in love, may have power, together with all the Lord's holy people, to grasp how wide and long and high and deep is the love of Christ, and to know this love that surpasses knowledge – that you may be filled to the measure of all the fullness of God' (Ephesians 3:17–19).

Love made known

We see that love of God revealed most clearly in Jesus. In him we see a life of humility, grace and perfect compassion. He had no regard for human values of pride and status but healed the sick, even touching lepers, preached good news to the poor, encouraged the rich to share their wealth, had compassion on the crowds that flocked to hear him even when he was tired and weary, and was counted a friend of 'sinners' – sitting with despised tax collectors and prostitutes.

He taught a standard of love which we find impossible, incredible or even ridiculous – love your enemies; if someone hits you, let them hit you again; if someone steals from you, give them something else to go with whatever they stole; pray for those who persecute you and bless those who hate you. Who else ever gave teaching like this and, more to the point, who could actually fulfil it?

These things were said in the context of Israel being occupied by the Roman army with punitive taxes to fund the Roman Empire, and people being captured and taken as slaves and often worked to death. They had enemies that it would be easy to hate. It was a Roman custom that their army could force local Jewish men to carry their baggage for one mile on their marches. Imagine how that would feel. This was the army occupying your country and brutalising and oppressing your people, and you were being asked to help them move their soldiers' equipment around to carry on their occupation. The Jews must have been incensed with anger and resentment at this practice, but Jesus taught that if they were asked to go one mile with them, they should go two![11] That would require superhuman grace, forgiveness and love.

Yet Jesus did not just teach like this, he also lived like it. He did not stand on his status as God, he did not retaliate or encourage others to retaliate on his behalf when insulted or abused, he did not fight back when beaten, and finally he prayed for the forgiveness of those nailing him to the cross.

---

[11] Matthew 5:39–41.

The beauty of his grace and humility is breathtaking. When he heals someone, even though it is his power that has healed them, he often says, 'Your faith has made you well.'[12] His first miracle is to turn water into wine at a wedding because his mother points out that they have run out of wine.[13] After centuries of preparation through the prophets, the Messiah has finally come into the world to save humanity, and surely his first public miracle will be to raise the dead, heal a multitude, feed the 5,000 – something spectacular and obviously holy? No, it is to turn water into wine at a local wedding! No wonder he says to Mary, 'What is that to you and to Me? My time… has not yet come' (John 2:4, AMP). Yet he goes on to do the miracle to provide the wine.

Imagine the first act of the incoming president of the USA was not some new, great national initiative for America, but to restock the wine cellar at the White House at the suggestion of his or her mother. They would become a laughing stock throughout the world. There is no way the President would comply with that suggestion because their concern for their public image would stop them. Jesus, however, graciously does the miracle out of compassion and respect for his mother, regardless of what it might look like.

Love your enemies. Jesus knew that Judas was stealing from the money donated for the disciples' food and other needs and that he would eventually betray him to his death,[14] but he did not treat him any differently than the

---

[12] For example Luke 17:19.

[13] John 2:1–11.

[14] John 12:6; John 6:70–71.

rest of his disciples. If I knew that our church treasurer was stealing from the church funds, I would be really angry and stop it immediately, but Jesus didn't. If I knew that someone was going to hand me over to be killed, even if I didn't run as far away as possible from him, I would find it incredibly difficult not to let it show that I didn't trust or like him. When at the last supper, Jesus says that one of the disciples will betray him, the others do not know who it is.[15] If he had treated Judas any differently to the rest, it would have been obvious to them who it was.

Whatever we might think that God would be like if we were to meet him in human form, maybe a great King surrounded by a glorious shining light and attended by armies of servants, we would never have imagined that he would be kneeling at our feet to wash the dirt and sweat from them,[16] or nailed in weakness to be tortured to death on a cross in our place. Yet this is the Son of God who loved us and came into the world not to 'be served, but to serve, and to give his life as a ransom for many' (Matthew 20:28). He didn't have to do it, he shrank back in horror from it, but he gave up his human life and faced the emptiness of losing God's love, a relationship that had existed from before the world was made, to take all our ugliness, sin, guilt and despair in order to rescue us from the destruction of a lost eternity.

Such amazing love, grace and humility! I've only scratched the surface but the disciples lived with him for more than three years and said that there was no sin in

---

[15] John 13:21–22.
[16] John 13:1–17.

him – never any selfishness, impatience, undue anger or irritability. At a distance lots of people can appear quite good, but when you live with someone, it is not long before you start to notice their minor faults and failings. Those who lived with Jesus saw none of that at all.

To spend time with Jesus would have been a completely unique experience because he was unlike anyone we have ever met before. He had no mask or pretended image, no concern about what people might think of him. He understood the hidden depths in the hearts of everyone he met, and had an overwhelming compassion and wisdom. He knew their past and their future fully, and to look into his eyes would be to come face to face with the Creator who made us and loves us more than we can now understand. Ten minutes with Jesus would and did change lives forever, and is literally better than a lifetime spent elsewhere.[17]

When I first read the Gospels, I was so moved by the person of Jesus that I would have lost my right arm to spend time with him. As soon as I realised that the good news was that through faith we could enter a living relationship with Jesus through his Spirit coming to live within us, and then walk with him throughout the rest of our lives and beyond, I wasted no time to offer myself and all I had to him.

This is the treasure beyond price – to know God through his Son Jesus, and his love in our lives now and forever. Can you see it? Can you feel it? To those of us who can see, the bright morning star, the spring of living

---

[17] Psalm 84:10.

water, he is the fragrance of life. He is worth more than anything else this world could ever offer.

But why is this hidden from so many?

3
Hidden in Plain Sight

The prophet Isaiah was inspired by God's Spirit to write, 'Truly you are a God who hides himself, O God and Saviour of Israel' (Isaiah 45:15, NIV 1984). The God who made the universe and whose power holds it all together has chosen to remain invisible within that universe. Over the centuries he has spoken directly to humanity, but relatively sparingly that we know about, and often in mysterious words and actions that are not easy to understand.[18]

Think of the detailed instructions for the Passover, Hosea being asked to marry a wife who would be unfaithful, the prophecies of Daniel, or Jacob wrestling with God. How were they understood by the people at the time? God often allows himself to appear weak or inactive, as in the suffering of Job or the 400 years of slavery of the Israelites in Egypt. There were about 400 years between the end of the Old Testament revelation and the coming of Jesus, and when he did come it was to a stable known to only a handful of people at the time. Why does God so often act this way when he could have

---

[18] Numbers 12:6; 2 Peter 3:16.

impressed us with a display of awesome power and given unmistakably clear proofs of his presence?

Parables

The Gospel record tells us that Jesus taught in parables – stories of everyday life which have a spiritual meaning – rather than straightforward, plain, easy-to-understand doctrine. Mark 4:34 tells us, 'He did not say anything to them without using a parable. But when he was alone with his own disciples, he explained everything.'

In Matthew 13, we find his disciples asking him why he was teaching like that. He had crowds of people in their thousands flocking to see him and hear what he had to say. He was healing all who came to him in faith and speaking with a wisdom and authority that the other religious leaders of the day did not share. Miracle followed miracle and the crowds kept coming. Imagine how many people would turn up at your local town hall or church if there was someone who could heal every blind person, make the lame walk and cure every sickness. He had an eager and enthusiastic audience, but he sent them away with everyday stories of local custom or agriculture, like a man who went out to sow seed and some was pecked up by birds, others grew just a little because of shallow soil or weeds and others grew well in good soil.

For most of the crowd, that – or parables like it – was all they heard. They came, saw some miracles, heard a story about a farmer or fishing or a wedding feast, and went home. The disciples realised that the crowd had not understood what Jesus said (and neither did they) and questioned him about what seemed to be a massive missed opportunity to reach the people with his teaching.

Jesus' response to their question is found in Matthew 13:11–16: 'the knowledge of the secrets of the kingdom of heaven has been given to you, but not to them. Whoever has will be given more, and he will have an abundance. Whoever does not have, even what he has will be taken from him. This is why I speak to them in parables: Though seeing, they do not see; though hearing, they do not hear or understand. In them is fulfilled the prophecy of Isaiah: "You will be ever hearing but never understanding; you will be ever seeing but never perceiving. For this people's heart has become calloused; they hardly hear with their ears, and they have closed their eyes. Otherwise they might see with their eyes, hear with their ears, understand with their hearts and turn, and I would heal them." But blessed are your eyes because they see, and your ears because they hear' (NIV 1984). What is Jesus saying here? He tells the disciples that he deliberately speaks to the crowds in parables because seeing they do not see, and hearing they do not hear, and he often ended his teaching with the rather strange command: 'He who has ears, let him hear.'[19] Everyone has ears, so what did he mean?

Most of the people in the crowds that came to see Jesus were simply curious to see a miracle or the latest holy man or prophet. They were not really interested in seriously seeking God and so were satisfied to see the

---

[19] For example, Matthew 11:15 (NIV 1984).

miracles, hear a nice story and return home with a tale to tell their family and friends. The amazing thing was that they had God himself there in their midst with all his power and wisdom, they saw and heard Jesus, but did not really see the significance of what he was saying. How many people both before and after the time of Jesus have longed for the chance to spend even a few minutes in his presence to listen to him, and yet most of those who were actually there did not realise the privilege they had. Jesus said that this was because their hearts were hard or calloused and so did not respond to the revelation of God's love in his words and in what he was doing.

When Jesus miraculously fed the 5,000, crowds came back the next day just looking for another free meal,[20] and Jesus started to say very difficult things that he knew they would not understand in order to send them away. He said that they had come looking for bread but that he was the true bread that came down from heaven, and they would have to eat his flesh and drink his blood to have real life. As soon as he talked like that, the crowds and even many of his disciples went away and stopped following him, but he meant that to happen!

Jesus used parables and hard teachings to sift the crowd, separating those who were really interested in seeking God from the majority who just wanted to see another miracle. John the Baptist had prophesied that the Messiah would sift God's people like threshing wheat to separate the grain which would be gathered into his barn from the chaff or shucks which would be burnt with

---

[20] John 6.

unquenchable fire.[21] John writes in his Gospel that God's light came into the world in Jesus and that people judge themselves by either coming to the light or shrinking back from it.[22]

So when his disciples came to ask him questions about the parables, Jesus said that the secrets of the kingdom of heaven had been given to them and he explained the parables to them. Why? *Because they had been interested enough to ask and not just to go home without understanding anything.*

He said that their eyes saw and their ears heard and because they had that heart to seek God, they would be given an abundance of life. Others whose hardness of heart meant that they failed to recognise the love and wisdom that Jesus was showing would never know the treasure of the kingdom of heaven. This is why God hides himself, sometimes appears weak or inactive, and reveals himself in often mysterious words and actions. He is a God of passionate love and is sifting out those who really love him and want to know him more.

God is looking for our hearts' response to his love

The whole message of the Bible can be summed up as a statement and a question. The statement is, 'I love you,' spoken in so many ways in creation, in God's plan for his people and in his loving message of goodness and salvation, but most of all expressed in action in Jesus

---

[21] Luke 3:17.
[22] John 3:19–21.

dying for us on the cross. The question is, 'Do you love me?' The most profound truth in the Bible is that God is love, and as creatures made in his image, he is looking for that response from us.

If God were to prove himself to us logically like a mathematical formula, then we would be compelled to believe in him intellectually, but that would not affect our hearts. If he gave undeniable signs of his presence daily to the whole world, it would win people's awe and respect but not necessarily their love, and if he forced us to believe and obey, then we would be puppets and would not be responding to him out of love. This has major implications for evangelism.

Paul puts it this way, in 1 Corinthians 1:21–25: 'For since in the wisdom of God the world through its wisdom did not know him, God was pleased through the foolishness of what was preached to save those who believe. Jews demand signs and Greeks look for wisdom, but we preach Christ crucified: a stumbling-block to Jews and foolishness to Gentiles, but to those whom God has called, both Jews and Greeks, Christ the power of God and the wisdom of God. For the foolishness of God is wiser than human wisdom, and the weakness of God is stronger than human strength.'

Ultimately it is not fine arguments or 'proofs' that bring people to salvation (although it is good to be ready to answer honest questions and give a reason for the hope that is in us[23]), and neither is it through seeing miracles (although miracles are signs of God being at work).

---

[23] 1 Peter 3:15.

Nobody had greater wisdom or had done more miracles than Jesus, but in the end the people did not believe him. The authorities had him put to death with the support of the crowds in Jerusalem, and his own disciples were disillusioned because they could not understand how it could all end that way.

No, it is the conviction of sin and the need of a saviour by the Holy Spirit, and the response to the revelation of God's love in the weakness and seeming foolishness of the cross where salvation was accomplished, that wins hearts for Jesus. God is looking for the response of our hearts to his love. In the Bible, God describes himself as a loving father or husband, choosing the closest and most intimate human relationships to describe how he feels about us. When we start to think about this, we can understand better why God treats us the way he does.

If a multi-billionaire had fallen in love, he would probably want to hide his wealth from his girlfriend to see whether she really loved him or was just interested in his money and lifestyle. If his wealth was obvious, it would be all too easy to attract the wrong kind of attention from someone pretending affection just to gain access to his riches. God is looking for a heart that warms to his love, not one that is just in awe of his power, and so he comes to a stable and not a palace, appearing weak rather than strong.

God invites us to seek him and to knock persistently on his door.[24] Seeking involves a process, someone who seeks searches diligently and does not usually find their

---

[24] Matthew 7:7–8.

desired object straight away. We find the same idea in Song of Songs 3:1–4: 'All night long on my bed I looked for the one my heart loves; I looked for him but did not find him. I will get up now and go about the city, through its streets and squares; I will search for the one my heart loves. So I looked for him but did not find him. The watchmen found me as they made their rounds in the city. "Have you seen the one my heart loves?" Scarcely had I passed them when I found the one my heart loves.'

There is a search going on here, and she does not immediately find her beloved. It is a common experience that when we set out to seek God's presence or guidance we don't necessarily find what we are looking for quickly. We may come back and back to times of prayer seemingly without any response from God, and then suddenly there is an answer. Why the delay?

If a man's son asks him for a piano and he gives it to him straight away, there is always a chance that he may play it for a little while and then lose interest in it. It was ultimately a waste of time and money. But if the boy has to wait and still shows enthusiasm for learning the piano and maybe gets a small job to save some money towards it, then there is much more certainty that he is really going to use it when he finally gets it. The wait actually makes it more appreciated and worthwhile, and also changes our attitude and behaviour as we wait. How many young lovers play 'Catch Me if You Can'? The search and chase demonstrate that the love they are pursuing means that much to them and heightens their anticipation of being with their beloved. God is encouraging us to develop our desire and longing for his love by making us wait for a touch of his presence.

Jesus said in Matthew 5:6, 'Blessed are those who hunger and thirst for righteousness, for they will be filled.' 'Hunger' and 'thirst' are strong words to describe a fierce longing for what is right. If we are really hungry, all we can think about is food, and if we are really thirsty, all we can think about is a drink. Is that how enthusiastic we are to search out and do what is right? We find the same sentiments for God's presence in the Psalms, for example in Psalm 42:1–2: 'As the deer pants for streams of water, so my soul pants for you, my God. My soul thirsts for God, for the living God. When can I go and meet with God?' Thirst will grow when we see a cool drink from a distance on a hot, dry day, and the drink will be savoured even more when we can eventually enjoy it.

But when we come to faith in Jesus and start a new life with him, why does God allow it to be so hard and difficult to follow him? We face temptation from within our own nature and from the world around us, and trouble and opposition, often from those closest to us, and from all the power of spiritual forces of evil in the world. We are usually highly outnumbered and outclassed in the spiritual war that we constantly face.

It is a common theme and storyline of ancient epic tales and modern novels and movies in every culture and society that boy meets girl, they face all kinds of difficulties, dangers and troubles, and then finally win through to be together. This is as true of Bollywood as Hollywood and of the *Ramayana* with Rama and Sita as the story of Robin Hood and Maid Marian. It would be a poor story and a boring movie if they just met and lived happily ever after. The troubles they go through and sacrifices they make to be together serve to deepen and define their love for one another. God loves us too much to allow us an easy, less passionate life!

There is a very strange story in Genesis 32 where Jacob wrestles with God as he is about to re-enter the promised land. A man meets him on the border and they wrestle all night because Jacob realises that he is more than a man and will not let him go until he blesses him. The man hurts him by wrenching his hip, causing him to limp afterwards. Still Jacob will not let go and finally gets his blessing, which is when his name is changed from Jacob (meaning 'deceiver') to Israel (meaning 'he wrestles with God').

This is a huge blessing because God then uses this name 'Israel' for his people throughout all time. When asked the most important of God's commandments about 2,000 years later, Jesus begins by quoting Moses: 'Hear O Israel: the Lord our God, the Lord is one' (Mark 12:29). In Galatians 6:16, Christians are called 'the Israel of God'. Imagine God was going to use your name to address his people for all time – what an amazing honour!

Of course, the name God gives us tells us something very profound about our relationship with him. 'He who wrestles with God'; not he who wrestles with the devil, the world or temptation, but he who wrestles with God. What does this mean?

In the story, Jacob believed so passionately in the value of the blessing that he was willing to persevere in wrestling, even after he was seriously hurt, to obtain it.

The treasure was worth all that he had, even his physical well-being. By not allowing our lives to be easy, God is bringing out of us how much we think he is worth to us. This is for our benefit primarily, as it challenges and then deepens our love for him. Is our love for God weak and shallow so that it disappears like the morning mist at the first sign of suffering or trouble? Will we continue to be faithful in difficult times when we do not understand what God is doing and he seems to have left the scene entirely? This is the whole message of the book of Job.

If there was a misunderstanding or difficulty between lovers, one might say to the other, 'Well, if that is all our love means to you, leave me then, if you want.' They are waiting to see if their love means more than the present trouble. We can see God acting like this with Jacob and in other parts of the Bible, and Jesus did the same. God knows, of course, the extent of our love for him, but he is eliciting a response from us so that we can experience what it means to really love him.

When all the crowds and many of his disciples left him in confusion and disbelief after his teaching on eating his flesh and drinking his blood, Jesus turned to the Twelve and asked them if they were going as well, knowing that they did not understand either. Peter replied, 'Lord, to whom shall we go? You have the words of eternal life' (John 6:68). He had eyes to see the treasure that was Jesus, even if he did not understand everything he said (and the disciples mostly did not understand until after Jesus' resurrection), and his journey of falling in love with him continued.

What do we see?

4
Veiled Eyes

Why is it that so many fail to recognise the treasure that is plain for all to see in Jesus? The Bible puts the answer this way in 2 Corinthians 4:2–4: 'setting forth the truth plainly we commend ourselves to everyone's conscience in the sight of God. And even if our gospel is veiled, it is veiled to those who are perishing. The god of this age has blinded the minds of unbelievers, so that they cannot see the light of the gospel that displays the glory of Christ, who is the image of God.' The 'god of this age', that is the devil, has put all kinds of diversions and distractions in our way to keep us from God if he can. Even Christians who have been born again into a new life can be so taken up with these that we end up losing out on the good things that God had otherwise planned to give us. What are these distractions?

The parable of the sower[25] outlines the main causes of the seed of the word of God failing to produce the harvest that it should in those who receive it. They are basically troubles, persecution, times of testing and the worries of this life, and love of money or other things. All of these

---

[25] Matthew 13:3–9, 18–23.

result in the little plant growing from the seed being unfruitful.

Fear of man and the troubles of life

Having been involved in pastoral ministry for more than 30 years, I am aware that it is common to find people who seemed to be running well in the Christian race but then drop out to sit by the race track when hurdles appear. Fear of the reaction of family, friends, workmates or the wider community can so easily paralyse any incentive to stand openly for Jesus, even to the point of stopping many from coming forward for baptism.

It is not for any us to sit in judgement over these things, for only God knows the pressures that each individual faces, and many who have had an easier life might have crumbled under harsher circumstances. We can only point to the many promises of God throughout the Old Testament and of Jesus in the New Testament to sustain and protect those in danger,[26] and his warnings against bowing to intimidation even from those nearest to us: 'Anyone who loves their father or mother more than me is not worthy of me; anyone who loves their son or daughter more than me is not worthy of me. Whoever does not take up their cross and follow me is not worthy of me. Whoever finds their life will lose it, and whoever loses their life for my sake will find it' (Matthew 10:37–39).

If the almighty living God is with us, then what do we have to fear? Not a hair on our head can be touched

---

[26] For example, Isaiah 41:10; Matthew 10:26–31.

without his permission, and our life is guaranteed until it is his time for us to die. Many times people tried to attack or even kill Jesus, but he just walked away and nothing could harm him until it was his time. The Roman governor, Pilate, angrily threatened him with the power to order his execution, but Jesus quietly said, 'You would have no power over me if it were not given to you from above' (John 19:11). God allows and limits whatever troubles or dangers we face, as he is actually in control of everything.[27]

By allowing conflict to occur within families – 'a man's enemies will be the members of his own household' (Matthew 10:36) – God is bringing out of us how much we think he is worth to us. Do we value God's love more than that of our wife, husband, parents or children? If so, is that just a little bit more, or is God our very heartbeat? What if it comes to a choice between loyalty to God or to family members? We will never know where we really stand until we face the test. Peter imagined that his loyalty to Jesus could stand up even to death threats, but found out the hard way that it wasn't as he thought on the night when Jesus was arrested.

Troubles come into our lives: unexpected illness, bereavement, failure at work or betrayal by loved ones. How do we react? Many react in anger or bitterness towards God and refuse to pray, read the Bible or go to church. 'Why has God allowed this to happen?' becomes the question they cannot get over, despite the clear teaching of Jesus that we would face many troubles in this

---

[27] 1 Corinthians 10:13.

world: 'In this world you will have trouble. But take heart! I have overcome the world' (John 16:33).[28] Again God is giving us opportunities to increase our faith by trusting him in difficult times and deepen our love for him by being faithful when we are in trouble.

Imagine a friend asks a favour that will take you considerable time and effort to fulfil. Life is good, you are feeling great, work is going well and home life is happy, and you carry out your friend's request. A few weeks later, the friend asks the same favour again but now you have a persistent headache, there is stress in the family home and your boss is disappointed with your work. You feel awful and just want to crawl away and hide, but you still do what your friend asked. Which occasion required the greater love for your friend? The second, of course!

God wants us to grow in love, and so he has to allow all kinds of troubles and difficulties to come our way so that we have the chance to exercise a greater faith and love.[29] He wants to produce mature disciples in the image of Jesus, not spiritual babies who run a mile as soon as the devil goes 'Boo!' This means *he loves us too much to give us an easy life*, as the difficulties and sufferings we face will be the means by which we mature in our love.

We need to keep our eyes fixed on Jesus[30] and what God is doing in our lives, and place our faith in him and his purposes. Otherwise our eyes will be blinded by the

---

[28] Read also Paul's description of a servant of God in 2 Corinthians 6:4–10.

[29] Romans 5:3–5; James 1:2–4.

[30] Hebrews 12:1–2.

immediacy of fear, and all we will see will be the dangers around us and not the loving hand directing our path.

What we truly value

We will treasure, worry about and work hard to achieve that which our hearts most value in life; often in this world that is money or what money can buy. It can also be wisdom or knowledge in an academic or intellectual career, or the pride and prestige that come from being successful or strong in any pursuit. These are the things that are normally valued in the world around us but can become stumbling blocks in the race to achieve really valuable treasure in heaven. God gives this warning in Jeremiah 9:23–24: 'Let not the wise boast of their wisdom or the strong boast of their strength or the rich boast of their riches, but let the one who boasts boast about this: that they have the understanding to know me, that I am the Lord, who exercises kindness, justice and righteousness on earth, for in these I delight.'

If our minds are concentrated on making money or achieving success at work to the exclusion of spending time seeking God or serving his people, then we have become blinded to the true values in life. When work, study or revision crowd out prayer, Bible reading and fellowship times, and when we neglect to prioritise church services in favour of visiting family, work shifts (if they could be rearranged) or pleasure activities, then we show by our actions what we really treasure above God.

We can give ourselves a quick test to assess our relative values. If we were promised a gift of £1,000 every time we attended a church service, prayer meeting or house group, how might we change our priorities in how we would organise our time? Would we suddenly find that we were able to get along to church and that we were not so busy after all? It is a fair guess that attendance at such meetings would quite amazingly flourish! But what would that say about what we really value? That money motivates us more than being with God? Actually, God's presence, love, joy and peace are infinitely more valuable than money, and if we would reorganise our time just for financial gain, how much more should we do it to prioritise time with him?

He makes his appeal to us in Isaiah 55:2: 'Why spend money on what is not bread, and your labour on what does not satisfy? Listen, listen to me, and eat what is good, and you will delight in the richest of fare.' God is saying that all these other things in life cannot ultimately satisfy the human heart, which was made in the image of God and can only find its fulfilment in his love. Do we hunger and thirst for his presence and what is right, or are our appetites being diverted elsewhere?

Truthfully, all these other priorities are self-serving, and if we are filled with the Holy Spirit and the love of God, we will be more concerned about the needs of others than about our own desires and ambitions. In his parable likening the kingdom of heaven to a treasure hidden in a field, the man who recognised the true value of the treasure rushed to sell everything he had with joy, in order to gain it. If we really see who Jesus is and our eyes are not veiled, then we will have no problem in fixing him as the number one priority in our lives. If we don't see, then our Christian lives will be stunted and fail to bear the fruit and harvest God is looking for.

In Jesus' time, those who saw the treasure had no hesitation in giving up their old ways to follow him. The fishermen Peter, Andrew, James and John left their nets, Matthew left his job collecting taxes, and crooked Zacchaeus immediately gave half of his possessions to the poor and repaid four times over anyone he had cheated. Paul gave up his position as an influential Pharisee to become an outcast from his Jewish community. Many have embraced poverty and danger down through the ages to become missionaries to spread the gospel message for the love of Jesus and the hope of a better inheritance in heaven. Their eyes could see.

William Carey left England in 1793 for missionary work in Calcutta, never to return to his homeland. He left behind everything familiar to go to a country about which he had only heard stories, where his wife would suffer a mental breakdown and where his eldest son would die at the age of 36. Sadhu Sundar Singh suffered the loss of his family who tried to poison him when he put his faith in Jesus. He took up the role of a 'sadhu', an itinerant preacher, living a simple life and travelling across north India, Afghanistan and Tibet barefoot in the early twentieth century with the gospel, becoming probably India's greatest preacher. Brother Yun – nicknamed 'the heavenly man' – and countless others suffered beatings and imprisonment by the Chinese authorities whilst seeing millions of Chinese turn to follow Jesus. Their eyes could see.

Others used their status and riches to serve God. William Wilberforce used his position in the British parliament to spend a lifetime campaigning for the abolition of slavery in the British Empire. The Countess of Huntingdon, a member of the eighteenth-century English aristocracy, used her rank and wealth to fund more than 64 chapels. It was said of her that she committed herself wholeheartedly to Christ's cause, not spending her money on herself, and refused to permit undue reverence to be paid to her because of her rank. Their eyes could see.

In Luke 8:18, just after the parable of the sower in Luke's Gospel, Jesus tells us to 'consider carefully' how we listen to him. Have we got eyes that see and ears that hear? Our response will determine our eternal destiny and how much we grow in his kingdom. Even the seed that fell into good soil produced differing harvests: some 'a hundred, sixty or thirty times what was sown'.[31]

How well are we growing in our most holy faith?

---

[31] Matthew 13:8.

5
Responsible to Grow

The idea of growth towards a harvest found in the parable of the sower is also in other parables of Jesus, where he describes the kingdom of God as being like a growing seed: 'It is like a mustard seed, which is the smallest of all seeds on earth. Yet when planted, it grows and becomes the largest of all garden plants, with such big branches that the birds can perch in its shade' (Mark 4:31–32). He chooses a tiny seed which you could hardly see on your finger to represent the unseen coming of the Holy Spirit into someone's heart. This seed then slowly grows to affect the whole local environment, providing shelter and shade. In the same way, our Christian lives should increasingly grow to provide a blessing to those around us, like a shady tree on a hot day.

It is clear that Jesus is teaching that the Christian life is about growth, and yet it is all too easy to think that once we are saved that is the end of the story. Some even say, 'Well, I'm saved now. I've got my place in heaven, nothing else matters.' There can be so much emphasis on what we have been saved *from* that we neglect what we have been saved *for*. It is true that the most important thing in this life is to receive God's forgiveness and eternal life by faith in Jesus, but that is the beginning of a new life, not the end.

When a baby is born, no one says, 'Great, he's a human being now. There's nothing more that needs to happen,' otherwise you would see a grown man on his hands and knees in nappies because he never learned to walk, talk, or perform any of the basics of life, let alone had a proper education to fulfil all his potential. Such a thing would be a tragedy! Yet somehow we can think it is fine for a new believer to remain a spiritual baby and never learn or grow nearer to God. No, God wants each of us to fulfil the potential he has put within us to be transformed into the mature image of Jesus.[32] He wants us to store up treasure in heaven and gain the fullness of the inheritance he has planned for us.

Jesus' picture of the tiny mustard seed growing into a tree (and the picture of God's people, Israel, as a fig tree, olive tree or vineyard in the Bible) is very encouraging, because it takes a human lifetime for a seed to grow into a tree. We can become very frustrated sometimes with our slow rate of growth in the Christian life, but we need to remember that a seed does not become a tree overnight, and a baby does not grow into a man or woman in a few days or even years.

Lifelong growth

Jesus told another parable about the kingdom of God, in Mark 4:26–29: 'A man scatters seed on the ground. Night

---

[32] 2 Corinthians 3:18.

and day, whether he sleeps or gets up, the seed sprouts and grows, though he does not know how. All by itself the soil produces corn – first the stalk, then the ear, then the full grain in the ear. As soon as the corn is ripe, he puts the sickle to it, because the harvest has come.' Here he is describing a process which occurs not by human power, and even without human understanding. God gives the growth and produces the harvest, but the farmer does need to water and weed the crop.[33]

When a seed is planted, at first a very small, fragile seedling pokes its leaves up above the soil. A brand-new believer often has a very basic grasp of the truths of the faith, and will often have many questions and struggles. The seedling needs water, light and protection, and the newborn believer needs the nourishment of God's word, prayer and fellowship: 'Like newborn babies, crave pure spiritual milk, so that by it you may grow up in your salvation' (1 Peter 2:2). Babies are not born knowing how to talk or walk, and new believers must learn how to pray and to walk by faith. It is only as babies grow that the world around begins to make more sense and they learn what is good for them and how to avoid dangers.

If you look at a baby from one day to the next, you will not see much difference, but if you come back in a year or two, you will notice how much they have grown. Similarly, if you look at a seedling from one day to the next, you might think it hasn't changed at all, but if you come back in a year or two, you will find a young plant. So it is with our Christian lives. We may not think we are

---

[33] 1 Corinthians 3:6–7.

growing much from day to day, but we can see the measure of change over time.

Young plants with weak stems and believers that are still young in the faith are vulnerable to being blown about by strong winds of change: 'Then we will no longer be infants, tossed back and forth by the waves, and blown here and there by every wind of teaching and by the cunning and craftiness of people in their deceitful scheming' (Ephesians 4:14). There are many sects and cults that subtly distort the teaching of the Bible, and sadly fads and fashions come and go in the Christian world as one aspect of truth or another is emphasised. The only sure foundation for growth is on the rock of putting into practice God's word.[34] Any other foundation will eventually prove as untrustworthy as shifting sand. As believers mature by understanding and following God's word, and the young plants gain a woody trunk, they become more stable and not so easily moved by the winds of 'new' teachings.

Maturity in the kingdom of God comes from a long process of faithful discipleship in prayerfully seeking God, learning from his word and walking in faith to fight temptation and do what is right. Hebrews 5:14 says that 'solid food is for the mature, who by constant use have trained themselves to distinguish good from evil'. It is only achieved by years of single-minded devotion. God gives us examples in 2 Timothy 2:4–6 of a soldier, athlete and farmer. The soldier does not get involved in civilian affairs, and we need to put aside anything that is a

---

[34] Matthew 7:24.

distraction to loving and serving God. The athlete competes according to the rules, and we have to live holy lives, not disregarding what God tells us to do. The farmer works hard to make sure that his crop is nourished and protected from pests, and we have to work hard to nourish our souls with God's word and weed out temptations to sin. In all of these examples, the desired result is not produced quickly or without a lot of sustained effort.

The idea that spiritual growth is the result of a lifelong, often slow and arduous process does not fit comfortably into our age of instant coffee, microwave meals that are ready in a few minutes, and ready access to the sum of human knowledge on the internet. We live with a world that moves faster and faster, where the attention span seems to be ever decreasing. Anything more than ten minutes and people are already losing interest. Consequently, we as Christians can often yearn for the 'quick fix' in our spiritual lives of some special prayer, new knowledge, experience or technique that will solve all our problems and instantly transform us into 'super-saints'. This is not the way God has designed things. There can be times of special blessing, miracles and great leaps forward in our understanding and walk with the Lord, but generally God wants to transform us bit by bit over a lifetime into the image of Jesus.

God spent many years maturing some of the great heroes of faith in the Bible. Abraham waited 25 years after he was first called for the birth of Isaac; Joseph spent years as a slave and then a prisoner before God exalted him to be Pharaoh's right-hand man; David from his teenage years served King Saul and then was persecuted by him until he became king at the age of 30; Paul started his first missionary journey with Barnabas after he had been a Christian for about 12 years; Moses was called at the age of 80! Given all of this, we can learn to be patient as we wait on the Lord to work out his will in our lives.

There is a beautiful picture of this in Proverbs 4:18: 'The path of the righteous is like the first gleam of dawn, shining ever brighter till the full light of day' (NIV 1984). When we first come to faith, the light of the love of God in our lives is like the first rays of sunlight at dawn, not very bright but with the promise of the coming day. No one doubts that the sun will come up, and God's settled will is for us to shine brighter and brighter as our lives progress. As we walk faithfully with him, more of his goodness shines through us and we see more of the spiritual reality around and within us, just as you see more of the surrounding landscape as the sun comes up. The movement of the sun across the sky is slow, almost imperceptible, but eventually the sun is shining in its full strength bringing light, heat and life to the land, and so eventually our walk with Jesus should bring light and life to others by his power at work within us. This is what God wills and wants to happen, but it is not always so.

The Master expects

If you have been following Jesus for a while now, it is a good exercise to look back over the last five years or so and see how you have been changing. It would be worrying to see no positive change at all over that period.

Jesus told various parables about a master who leaves his servants to go away on a journey. He is gone a long time but eventually returns to see how faithful his servants have been whilst he was away, looking for fruit from his vineyard or a return on his money. Probably the most famous of these parables is called the parable of the talents.[35] Likewise, it is clear that God is going to call us to account one day for all he has given us, and he will be looking for the spiritual harvest of our lives.

In the parable of the talents, the master leaves his servants with different amounts of money. This is interesting as it seems to be confirming what we all know, that the world is not a level playing field – some people have many more advantages than others. Some are born into rich families, receive a good education and live a fairly trouble-free life, whilst others in this world live in poverty, maybe abandoned by their parents, or try to survive in the midst of terrible war zones. Some have loving Christian parents who bring them up to love the Scriptures and come to faith at an early age; others face implacable opposition, violence or even death threats from their family or community if they want to follow Jesus. Some are born physically and mentally healthy and strong, whilst others face a lifetime of struggling with physical or mental disability or pain.

No, it's not fair, but God is fair as he practises the principle, 'From everyone who has been given much, much will be demanded; and from the one who has been entrusted with much, much more will be asked' (Luke

---

[35] Matthew 25:14–30.

12:48). The servant who started with two talents was expected to make only two more, whilst the servant who started with five talents was expected to make five more. Although at the end, one has four talents whilst the other has ten, the master is equally happy with them both and the wording of his commendation to them is identical.[36]

This has profound implications about how we look at life. First of all, it shows the futility of comparing ourselves to each other, as only God knows the advantages and handicaps that each person faces. Only God can judge how faithful a person has really been in their service as only he knows the struggles and difficulties they had to overcome to serve him. It also means that we can relax about the unfairness of this world, knowing that God will judge all things fairly and justly in the end.

Our Christian lives should have a graph of spiritual growth that looks something like this:

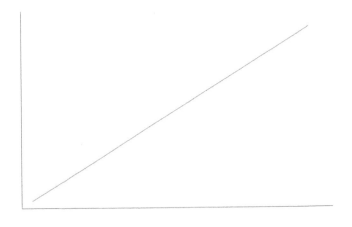

---

[36] Matthew 25:21, 23.

But may instead look something like this:

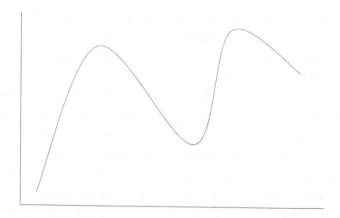

Or like this:

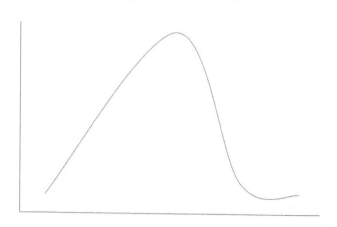

Or perhaps like this:

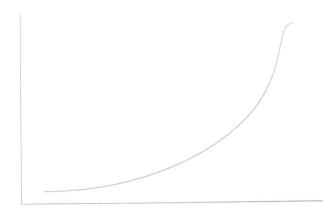

Most people start their Christian lives with a 'honeymoon' period, fed by their initial faith and love for the Lord Jesus. In the parable of the sower in Matthew 13, even the seeds that fall into shallow soil and amongst weeds start to grow well, but then persecution or trouble arises or the distractions of the world stunt the growth. Sadly, we can all too easily allow ourselves to take the things of the Lord for granted as time goes on, and our Christian life deteriorates into a routine void of any real passion. There is no longer a hunger and thirst for his presence or a desire to seek his will because we have allowed ourselves to become distracted and weighed down by the concerns of this life. If this happens, our growth plateaus out or even declines. We become vulnerable to taking our eyes off the Lord and falling into the devil's traps and temptations.

King Solomon started out well, asking the Lord for wisdom to rule for the good of the people rather than asking for wealth, honour or the death of his enemies. He went on to build and dedicate the temple in Jerusalem and to rule with legendary justice. God gave him wisdom beyond that of any other man, and his wise sayings inspired by God ring true 3,000 years later, in the books of Proverbs and Ecclesiastes. But his spiritual walk did not end well. The temptation of women and the desire to make political alliances through marriage (rather than have faith in God's protection) led him to marry many foreign wives in direct disobedience to the Law of Moses.[37] These foreign wives then put pressure on him to build temples for their idols in Jerusalem and even for him to follow their gods with them. God was so offended that he allowed Solomon's empire and physical legacy to collapse on his death.

Our only hope of running the race set out before us faithfully to the end to win the prize is to keep our eyes fixed in faith on Jesus. He started us out on the track and will keep us till the end as we trust in him.[38]

What would the graph of our Christian lives look like so far?

---

[37] Deuteronomy 7:3–4; 17:17.
[38] Hebrews 12:1–2.

6
Not by Works

At this point some may be thinking that all this sounds like a great burden being placed on our shoulders to run the race God has laid out for us, and to build treasure in heaven. Yet Jesus said that his yoke was easy and his burden was light,[39] and so we need to remind ourselves of the basics of the gospel to focus our minds on this.

Dead in sin

The Bible tells us that we were 'dead in … transgressions and sins' (Ephesians 2:1) before we put our trust in Jesus and were born again by the Holy Spirit. A dead person is not able to do anything, and this is literally saying that without the transforming power of a new creation giving us a new heart through faith in Christ, we cannot do anything truly righteous. We do not just commit sins, we are sinners by nature, born with instincts for selfishness, greed, pride and lust and so on, and incapable of pleasing God: 'the sinful mind is hostile to God. It does not submit to God's law, nor can it do so. Those controlled by the

---

[39] Matthew 11:30.

sinful nature cannot please God' (Romans 8:7–8, NIV 1984).

Are we really born sinners?[40] Aren't little children good at heart until they are corrupted by the world around them? Well, which parent ever has to teach their toddler to be selfish or demand their own way, to get angry when they are denied their every wish, or to grab something they want from another toddler and fight them for it if necessary? They do these things automatically, and we teach them to be kind to one another and to share. It was once thought that toddlers pick up how to lie from adults, but most parents know that if there is a mess on the floor with a little one in the middle of it covered with goo, the question, 'Did you do that?' will be met with the answer, 'No!' Lying requires no training.

Our innate selfishness and greed may start with food and toys but will later move on to money, possessions and power. Pride and envy, too, seem to be inborn. Watch toddlers if you show attention to one and ignore the other. The one that has been ignored often gets angry with the one who had the attention, and may even hit them. This progresses later to seeking status by comparing ourselves with each other in terms of wealth or careers, and to nations going to war over the honour of their country.

Even our best acts of human kindness and goodness are tainted by our selfish, human nature, with mixed motives and hints of self-satisfaction or pride. It is very hard not to want our good deeds to be noticed and appreciated and not to become proud of our so-called

---

[40] Psalm 51:5.

humility! The prophet Isaiah says 'all our righteous acts are like filthy rags' (64:6), and so our human attempts at good deeds are not acceptable in God's sight.

Of course, if God's standard is perfection[41] and his commands are that we should love him with all that we are and love each other as much as he has loved us,[42] then who could ever say that they have kept his commands faithfully for even one day or hour? No, we do not please God, grow in our Christian lives or gain treasure in heaven by trying to act in our strength, but by trusting in Christ's power at work within us. Jesus said that without him we could achieve nothing of any spiritual value,[43] and in Paul's letter to the Church in Rome we find the shocking statement, 'everything that does not come from faith is sin' (Romans 14:23).

The righteous shall live by faith

Like salvation, a righteous life is only achieved by faith,[44] and the Bible tells us, 'The only thing that counts is faith expressing itself through love' (Galatians 5:6). In order to live a life acceptable to God, we need to deny ourselves, put to death our old nature and trust Jesus to live in us moment by moment. Paul says in Galatians 2:20, 'I have been crucified with Christ and I no longer live, but Christ lives in me. The life I now live in the body, I live by faith

---

[41] Matthew 5:48.

[42] Matthew 22:37–40; John 13:34.

[43] John 15:5.

[44] Romans 1:17.

in the Son of God, who loved me and gave himself for me.'

The amazing truth is that the Christian life is not just difficult for us to live, it is impossible! In fact, God is not impressed by anything that is possible for us to do ourselves because that would just be the product of our human nature. He is only interested in the impossible! Having watched a rich young man walk away rather than sell all his possessions to give to the poor, the disciples asked Jesus how anyone could be saved. He replied, 'With man this is impossible, but with God all things are possible' (Matthew 19:26).

The story in Matthew's Gospel of Jesus walking on the water[45] really illustrates this. The disciples were battling against the wind and the waves on Lake Galilee in the middle of the night and suddenly Jesus approached the boat, walking on the water. After their initial shock, thinking it was a ghost, they recognised Jesus, and Peter asked Jesus to call him to come to him on the water. The previous day, Jesus had told them to give more than 5,000 people something to eat when they only had five loaves and two fish. Absolutely impossible, but when Jesus gave thanks suddenly there was more than enough food for everyone, and he had given the disciples the ability to feed the people. So Peter had the amazing faith to believe that if Jesus commanded him to walk on the water, he would give him the power to do it.

Peter stepped out of the boat, and as long as he was trusting in Jesus, he walked on the water, but when he

---

[45] Matthew 14:22–33.

started to look at the waves and felt the wind, he began to think that this was impossible and began to sink. Jesus reached over and pulled him up into the boat saying, 'You of little faith, why did you doubt?'

The lesson for us is clear. Jesus' commands to us are just as impossible for human nature to carry out as walking on the water: love your enemies; if someone hits you, let them hit you again; if someone steals something from you, give them something else to go with it; always be patient; always be kind; rejoice in all circumstances. Faced with demands like this, our initial reaction can be, 'You've got to be kidding me!' We can only fulfil these commands if we fix our faith on Jesus to fill us with his Spirit and give us the power to live the way he wants us to live. If we trust in him, we find the miracle occurs and we can say with Paul, 'I can do everything through him who gives me strength' (Philippians 4:13, NIV 1984). As soon as we focus on our circumstances, however, we sink like Peter, and we fail.

In John 15, Jesus describes himself as a vine and says that we are the branches. Obviously any branch that is cut off from the vine will wither and die, and only those branches attached to the vine receiving the life-giving sap will be able to stay alive and bear fruit. In the same way, it is only when we are filled with the supernatural life of God's Holy Spirit that we are able to bear fruit for God and act in a way that is acceptable to him. Jesus says in John 15:5, 'apart from me you can do nothing'. Our aim should be to say with Paul, 'I no longer live, but Christ lives in me' (Galatians 2:20).

It is only as we live in the power of God's Spirit that we achieve anything of spiritual worth that will count towards treasure in heaven. Let us look again at that passage in Galatians 6:7–9: 'Do not be deceived: God cannot be mocked. A man reaps what he sows. The one who sows to please his sinful nature, from that nature will reap destruction; the one who sows to please the Spirit, from the Spirit will reap eternal life. Let us not become weary in doing good, for at the proper time we will reap a harvest if we do not give up' (NIV 1984). This is warning us that only what is done in the power of the Holy Spirit brings a harvest to eternal life. Whatever is done simply by our own human nature is destined for destruction because it does not meet God's holy standard.

We find the same idea in 1 Corinthians 3:11–15: 'For no one can lay any foundation other than the one already laid, which is Jesus Christ. If anyone builds on this foundation using gold, silver, costly stones, wood, hay or straw, their work will be shown for what it is, because the Day will bring it to light. It will be revealed with fire, and the fire will test the quality of each person's work. If what has been built survives, the builder will receive a reward. If it is burned up, the builder will suffer loss but yet will be saved – even though only as one escaping through the flames.'

The foundation of our Christian lives is the death and resurrection of Jesus, and obtaining forgiveness of sins and new life through faith in him. How we build on that foundation, what we do with the great gift of salvation that has been given to us, will then determine what reward/treasure we are to receive in heaven; not by works but by exercising faith to live by the power of the Holy Spirit, rather than in our own strength.

The gold, silver and costly stones, which would survive fire, represent deeds done by faith in the power of the Spirit whilst the wood, hay and straw, which would of course be burnt, represent the works of our human nature. Fire in the Bible often represents God's holiness, and so on Judgement Day each person's life will be tested by the burning purity of God's holiness. Whatever has been done by the Spirit will survive and be rewarded, but whatever has not will be destroyed, although the person themselves will be saved, because our forgiveness and salvation have been won for us by Jesus on the cross and do not depend on anything we do.

The danger is that if we come from a privileged background and have been born with a well-rounded, easy disposition, we might settle for a nice, decent, comfortable Christian life lived in our own strength, without actually seeking and living in the supernatural, humanly impossible love of God. The Christian life must be supernatural to mean anything to God.

It would be a terrible loss to arrive in heaven and look back to see all that we thought we had achieved in life become dust and ashes: all our material gains, whatever wealth and collections of precious possessions we had amassed, and the pride that we took in our career, family or even work for God rendered meaningless and a waste of time and effort. This is serious stuff and something we should fervently and prayerfully seek God about with the utmost passion, lest our eyes be blinded by the distractions of the world and we waste the life he has given us and lose the reward and inheritance he wanted us to have.

Are we living by faith that Jesus lives in us, or mostly by our own human nature?

7

According to Our Deeds

It is clear throughout the Bible that God's judgement is according to what a person has done. Revelation 20:12 tells us, 'The dead were judged according to what they had done,' and in Romans 2:6–8 we read, 'God "will repay each person according to what they have done." To those who by persistence in doing good seek glory, honour and immortality, he will give eternal life. But for those who are self-seeking and reject the truth and follow evil, there will be wrath and anger.'[46]

The grace that comes through Jesus frees us from the condemnation of judgement by forgiving our sins and gifting us with the righteousness of God himself in Christ.[47] It is the only foundation for building a life with God, and it means that we do not come into the final judgement before God because our punishment already fell on Jesus who died in our place. Trusting in Jesus means that we are not under God's condemnation, will not pay for our sins and are in no danger of punishment in hell.

---

46 Psalm 62:12; Proverbs 24:12.

47 Romans 3:20–24.

As Christians brought from death to eternal life, however, 'We must all appear before the judgement seat of Christ, so that each of us may receive what is due to us for the things done while in the body, whether good or bad' (2 Corinthians 5:10).[48] Jesus will assess how we have lived our lives and reward us or not accordingly. What an awesome thought! We will all have a personal interview with Jesus to go over what we have done with all he has given us.

Right now we do not fully understand the mystery of what happened at the cross or grasp the vast extent of how much God loves us, but when we come face to face with Jesus we will know him completely, even as we have been fully known.[49] Imagine seeing for the first time the scars in his hands and feet, and our minds being opened to the scale of the spiritual agony and loss that he faced on our behalf in order to save us – how much he loved us to go into the despair of eternal darkness, cut off from the Father's love for our sake.

Imagine realising all of that for the first time and then thinking, 'But what did I do for him?' as you looked back on a life lived selfishly, ignoring his love and neglecting the plan he had laid down before the world was made to bless you and make you a blessing to others. As a loving Father he planned every detail of a race for us to run, battles for us to fight, glory for us to win, because he wanted us to be the best possible creature we could be,[50] and we let it all slip between our fingers. It would be so

---

[48] Colossians 3:23–25.

[49] 1 Corinthians 13:12.

[50] Ephesians 2:10.

72

sad to hear, 'My precious child, there was so much I wanted you to do and to bless you with, but you were too interested in the things of that lost world.'

If a child knew that their parents had sacrificed much, scraped and saved and gone without, to send them to get educated in a foreign land, but did nothing for them in return, how would they feel when their parents died? Perhaps they meant to go and visit them over the years or to phone more often, but somehow they were always too busy with their studies and career and spending time with their friends. Now the parents are dead and there is no more opportunity to do anything for them, or to show appreciation for all they did. Once we are in heaven, there are no more battles to fight for God, no more struggles with temptation or difficult times in which to be faithful – no more opportunities to demonstrate our love for him in this way.

Faced with this sobering truth that we will all individually appear before Jesus, Paul says in 2 Corinthians 5:9 and 11: 'So we make it our goal to please him … Since, then, we know what it is to fear the Lord, we try to persuade others.'

All this leaves us with another astounding implication: that heaven is not a uniform or equal experience for all those there (and neither is hell). The very fact of the opportunity to build treasure in heaven or not necessitates differing outcomes. Furthermore, the Bible clearly teaches that not all sin is equal. There are differing levels of darkness and punishment for those who reject God's love and grace in salvation.

The depths of hell

James 2:10–11 says, 'For whoever keeps the whole law and yet stumbles at just one point is guilty of breaking all of it. For he who said, "You shall not commit adultery," also said, "You shall not murder." If you do not commit adultery but do commit murder, you become a law-breaker.' These verses are sometimes quoted as teaching that all sin is the same and that a temper tantrum is as bad as murder, and fiddling your taxes as bad as genocide. This can then be used to justify going on to commit a worse sin after a minor one (such as actually committing adultery after being taken up with lust) as, after all, they are just as bad! This is not what James is saying, however. Rather, he is showing that whatever sin we commit is enough to make us a law-breaker and therefore guilty before God. The smallest sin would be enough to keep us out of heaven as we would have fallen short of God's perfect standards and would have broken his law.

Of course, saying an unkind word is not as bad as murder; both are wrong but they are not the same! Lustful thoughts are sinful but not as bad as actually acting on them. Jesus says in Matthew 5:28 that 'anyone who looks at a woman lustfully has already committed adultery with her *in his heart'* (my italics) – not in outward deed. The whole point of his teaching is not to say that there is no difference between thoughts and actions, but rather to say that both matter and will alike be judged by God. The punishments in the Law of Moses varied from fines of compensation to beatings, and from exclusion from the community right up to even death, depending on the severity of the sin involved. God did not and does not view all sin as equally bad.

Jesus criticised the Jewish religious leaders for concentrating on minor issues of the law, like tithing the herbs from their gardens whilst neglecting the more important matters of justice, mercy and faithfulness. He said that they would 'strain out a gnat but swallow a camel' (Matthew 23:23–24), being so concerned about small outward things that people could see but ignoring the attitudes of the heart, and so becoming like whitewashed tombs that might look good from the outside but were full of corruption on the inside.[51]

Jesus also pointed out that knowingly doing something wrong is worse than doing it unwittingly, and that the punishment for such sins differs. Luke 12:47–48: 'The servant who knows the master's will and does not get ready or does not do what the master wants will be beaten with many blows. But the one who does not know and does things deserving punishment will be beaten with few blows.' This is an important principle as it means that judgement is stricter for those who have had more light and grace given to them by God.

The towns in which Jesus performed most of his miracles came in for particular criticism because they did not change their lives even after seeing so much of God's power at work: 'Woe to you, Chorazin! Woe to you, Bethsaida! For if the miracles that were performed in you had been performed in Tyre and Sidon, they would have repented long ago in sackcloth and ashes. But I tell you, it

---

[51] Matthew 23:27.

will be more bearable for Tyre and Sidon on the day of judgment than for you. And you, Capernaum, will you be lifted to the heavens? No, you will go down to Hades. For if the miracles that were performed in you had been performed in Sodom, it would have remained to this day. But I tell you that it will be more bearable for Sodom on the day of judgment than for you' (Matthew 11:21–24).

These words must have cut right through the residents of these Jewish towns, as they would have considered themselves, as followers of the one true God, morally superior to the idol worshippers of Tyre and Sidon. Also, Sodom was notorious in the Old Testament as an example of God's extreme judgement, being destroyed by fire from heaven because of the depth of its sexual immorality, without even ten righteous people within it.[52] For them to be told that they would fare worse on the day of judgement than Tyre, Sidon and Sodom would have been profoundly shocking.

But they had experienced God incarnate amongst them performing signs and wonders, teaching with perfect wisdom and living out his love and goodness. To remain unmoved by it all demonstrated such a hardness of heart that it became an outrage against God's love and an insult to his grace. It is a far worse thing for people to turn their back on Jesus having known something of his power and love than for those who have not heard about him,[53] because it is like looking love right in the eye and saying, 'No.'

---

[52] Genesis 18:20–19:26.
[53] 2 Peter 2:20–21; Hebrews 10:26–31.

So it is clear that sin has its depths of depravity and hell its deeper darkness for those who deliberately suppress and ignore the light of God's love. Similarly, there are degrees of reward in heaven.

The heights of heaven

Jesus told a parable about a landowner who hired workers at different times to work that day in his vineyard. Some he hired early in the morning and others throughout the day, even up to one hour before pay time. When it came to giving them their wages, he paid them all equally. The ones who had been hired early in the day then complained that it was unfair that they had been made equal to those who came late.[54]

This parable is sometimes used to argue that the rewards in heaven are all equal for everyone, but in the Jewish mind, the vineyard would represent Israel and the first workers would be the Jewish people.[55] The parable addresses the surprise and maybe resentment that Jews would feel that God would give the gift of salvation and entry into the promised kingdom of heaven equally to recently converted Gentiles as to Jews who had been worshipping God for centuries (Jesus had commended the faith of a Roman centurion and accepted Samaritan followers). Similarly, the gift of God's forgiveness and eternal life remains the same whether we come to faith in

---

[54] Matthew 20:1–16.

[55] Isaiah 5:1–7; Matthew 21:33–45.

Jesus in our youth or on our deathbed; it is not dependent on how long we have been following him.

Throughout the Gospels, however, Jesus makes statements about relative rewards in heaven. He says that there is great reward for being persecuted for his sake, Matthew 5:11–12: 'Blessed are you when people insult you, persecute you and falsely say all kinds of evil against you because of me. Rejoice and be glad, because great is your reward in heaven'; and for loving your enemies, Luke 6:35: 'Love your enemies, do good to them, and lend to them without expecting to get anything back. Then your reward will be great, and you will be children of the Most High.'

In Mark 10, we find teaching linking rewards in heaven to sacrifice and service. Mark 10:29–30 says that 'no one who has left home or brothers or sisters or mother or father or children or fields for me and the gospel will fail to receive a hundred times as much in this present age: homes, brothers, sisters, mothers, children and fields – along with persecutions – and in the age to come eternal life', and Mark 10:43–44 explains, 'whoever wants to become great among you must be your servant, and whoever wants to be first must be slave of all'. It is clear that rewards in heaven reflect the service that has been offered to God.

The areas which God allocated as inheritance in the promised land to each of 11 out of the 12 tribes of Israel were not equal, and the inheritance of the tribe of Levi was to be God himself, so they were not given any land. This was a privilege for the Levites (as a reward for their loyalty during the time when the Israelites had worshipped the golden calf[56]) because God is a better inheritance than land and those who were priests could serve near to God in the tabernacle/temple. This was a physical, visual aid representing our journey to our inheritance in the promised land of heaven and is meant to help inspire us in our efforts to build treasure there.

A father has many children and he loves them all equally. He has no favourites, but some of them spend time with him whilst others are distracted by other things. When they are young, some of them sit on his lap and listen to his stories, they leap into his arms for a cuddle and follow him everywhere. The others are more interested in their computer games or in going out to play with their friends. As they grow older, the first group take an interest in the family business, trying to learn as much as they can from their father as to how he runs things, whilst their other brothers and sisters pursue their own careers and spend their leisure time holidaying away from home. Which of this man's children will know him better?

When Jesus was visiting the house of one of the Pharisees, a local woman who had lived an immoral life came in and started to weep and to wash his feet with her tears.[57] The guests and host were surprised and outraged, but Jesus asked his host a question. He said that two people owed money: one owed 500 denarii and the other 50. If the debts of both were written off, which one would love their creditor more? The host answered that it was obviously the one who had owed the bigger debt.

---

[56] Exodus 32:26–29; Numbers 18:20–24.

[57] Luke 7:36–50.

So it is that the more we understand the extent of God's grace in forgiving our sins in Jesus' death on the cross, the more we will love him, and the more we love him, the more ecstatic in worship we will be in his presence. It is a paradox that the more we grow in the Christian life and see God's standards of goodness more clearly, the more convinced we become of our own sinfulness and lack of holiness, but the more grateful and thankful we become towards God. The bad news is that we are much more sinful than we think, but the good news is that God loves us anyway, and his grace and unearned forgiveness and blessings are greater still.

It is clear in the description of heaven in the book of Revelation that some are nearer to God than others. The throne of God is said to be surrounded by four living creatures and 24 elders, and a group of human beings is described as following Jesus wherever he goes and being especially near to him. They know a special song that they sing to God which no one else knows, and this suggests a more intimate understanding and love for God.[58]

God has no favourites amongst his children, but we determine how near to him we come by our response to his love. Someone once said, 'Everyone can be as holy as they want to be.' As we have already seen, God is our greatest treasure in heaven, and we will set our own limits on that reward.

Are we reaching for the heights?

---

[58] Revelation 14:1–5.

8
Kingdom Economics

Worldly economics, the working of the stock market and the laws of supply and demand, basically depend on two facets of human nature – fear and greed. The motivation of greed to make more and more profits drives share prices up as people buy increasingly in a rising market, hoping to boost their wealth as the price of the shares they have bought rises. This happens until a turning point of confidence occurs, when most people think that the price cannot reasonably rise any further, and then they start to sell the shares to cash in their profits, causing the price to start to fall. Fear then hits the market and floods of people sell to get out with their money whilst they can. The trick, of course, is to buy when the price is low and sell when it is high!

The economics of God's kingdom is entirely different and sets the world's values upside down. The world would say that we are blessed if we are rich, happy, powerful, self-sufficient and popular, but Jesus says that we are blessed if we are poor in spirit, in mourning over the state of our souls and the world around us, meek, hungering and thirsting for what is right, and persecuted for righteousness.[59]

Clearly, the kingdom of God works in a radically different manner to the world we live in. This world rewards the rich, powerful and strong, but God rewards the kind, loving and righteous.

Love is all

The most profound and definitive statement about God is found in 1 John 4:8: 'God is love'. Everything in his kingdom revolves around this truth. It is his love for us that caused God to choose us before the universe was created, bring us into being, and send Jesus to die in our place in order to save us and recreate us into a new relationship with him,[60] and it is our understanding of his love that will cause us to love him more and to love one another: 'This is love: not that we loved God, but that he loved us and sent his Son as an atoning sacrifice for our sins. Dear friends, since God so loved us, we also ought to love one another' (1 John 4:10–11).

God has revealed his love to us in many ways in the Bible, telling us that his love for us is as high as the stars are above the earth and that he loved us in eternity before the universe was made and that he always will.[61] Light can travel 100 million miles in about eight minutes, but it would take it about four years to reach the nearest star, around two million years to reach our neighbouring

---

[59] Matthew 5:3–10.

[60] Ephesians 1:4–5.

[61] Psalm 103:11, 17.

Andromeda galaxy, and billions of years to reach the most distant galaxies. These are unimaginable distances, and then God says that his love for us is greater than that, and that he loved us before those stars and galaxies started to shine that light and will always love us, long after they have gone out! Like the moon and the stars in the sky, his love for us never changes and his coming to our side is as sure as the sun rising.

God says that he takes care of every hair on our heads, knows every word before we say it and is watching over us when we get up, go out, come in and go to bed. He knew us before we were born and knows every day of our lives from beginning to end. He says that his thoughts about us outnumber the grains of sand![62] Think how many grains there would be in just a glass full of sand and then the number on all the beaches of the world – awesome!

He gives us a picture of an old man, Abraham, taking his only beloved son, Isaac, to sacrifice him on Mount Moriah in loving obedience to God, and at the last minute we all breathe a sigh of relief when the angel of the Lord intervenes to tell Abraham not to do it but to sacrifice a nearby ram instead.[63] We can all relate to the heartache that old man must have gone through to plan out a three-day journey to Moriah, put the wood for the sacrifice on his son's back and hear the boy's questions, asking, 'Where is the sacrifice?', and then to tie him up and raise the knife. What is that all about?

---

[62] Luke 12:7; Psalm 139.
[63] Genesis 22:1–19.

Well, about 2,000 years later, God's only Son, Jesus, is standing on that same Mount Moriah, where Solomon built the Jewish temple, saying that he had come not 'to be served, but to serve, and to give his life as a ransom for many' (Mark 10:45). There was no one to tell God to stop, and he planned out in agony of heart for Jesus to be sacrificed on that hill because he loved us. It was not Abraham's only son, but it was God's only Son that was to be the sacrifice, and that whole Genesis story (right down to Isaac carrying the wood for the sacrifice as Jesus would one day carry the cross) is God communicating to us a bit of what it was like for him to take Jesus to the cross in order to save us. How much he must love us to do that!

He gives us another picture of an older brother, Judah, an ancestor of Jesus, offering himself to become a slave and take the punishment of his younger brother, Benjamin, because his elderly father's life was so tied up in his love for Benjamin that it would kill him if he didn't come home.[64] God the Father is telling us that this is how much he loves us, and is a picture of Jesus, our older brother, offering himself to take our punishment in our place.

Who would not love such a God? No wonder a friend of mine, when asked what he was doing reading the Bible in the library, said that he was reading his love letters! If we understand God's love for us, we will think nothing of spending hours and hours with him in prayer and reading his love letters to us. Think of how many hours a

---

[64] Genesis 44:17–34.

boy and girl will spend on the phone or Skype to each other. If you were to question that as a waste of time, they would laugh because they love each other and are thrilled with each other's company. How much do we know of God's love, and how much do we therefore experience and value it?

Jesus asked us to regularly remember his death for us by sharing the bread and cup of communion.[65] The cross is the main way that God has demonstrated his love for us,[66] and although it is hard for us to grasp what it meant for a pure and holy God to take upon himself all the ugliness, guilt and horror of the world's evil, we *can* understand a man dying a torturous death nailed to a cross. The physical suffering of Jesus' beatings, whippings and crucifixion can evoke our human emotions, but the real agony was actually when he was cut off from the eternal love of God the Father and he cried out, 'My God, my God, why have you forsaken me?' (Matthew 27:46).

Imagine a happily married couple who are atheists. They have lived together for more than 60 years and although it was not perfect, they had a really fantastic love for each other. Now, however, he is stood by his wife's graveside and everything they had between them is gone. He doesn't believe in life after death and so there is no hope, no way back; their love is forever lost and over.

Take that loveless darkness and add in all the guilt and horror of every murderer, rapist, tyrant and torturer, the trapped lust of the addict, the callous arrogance of the oppressor and the petty pride and selfishness of billions

---

65 Luke 22:19.

66 1 John 3:16.

of human beings. That is as near as we can get to imagining hell, and Jesus faced the totality of that for us all. Although he was only a few hours on the cross, God is outside time, and 'with the Lord a day is like a thousand years' (2 Peter 3:8). Wouldn't it have seemed like eternity to him? Outside of time, everything is now and the Bible talks about 'the Lamb who was slain from the creation of the world' (Revelation 13:8).

The worst punishment that we have, short of the death penalty, is to put someone into solitary confinement. Without any human contact, a person's psyche begins to disintegrate and many lose their grip on reality and go mad. It is said that even if someone is being tortured, they often prefer that to the days of isolation as at least there is some human presence. We are creatures made in the image of our Creator God of love, and without any prospect of love, life is no longer worth living. That too is a glimpse of hell, which Jesus referred to in Matthew's Gospel as the 'outer darkness' (Matthew 25:30, NKJV), and which he suffered on our behalf. He had shared a perfect love with God the Father from all eternity, and he was shut out in the darkness on the cross for our sake.

If a close friend had dived in front of a car to save you and ended up getting killed, you would always remember them. You might have a photo of them somewhere and whenever you looked at that picture, it would touch your heart. That person might have been alive now, and not you; they might have got married and had children but gave it all up to save you. Let us meditate in faith on the love of God for us in Jesus being tortured to death and taking all our sin, guilt, loneliness and despair upon himself so that we might never face it ourselves. He did not have to do it; he did it because he loved us so much and could not bear to lose us.

This is the meaning of sharing the bread and the cup in communion, because as we take those physical symbols, they remind us again and again of God's great love for us, which should in turn reignite our love for him. If we remain cold in the face of such love, we really need to get on our knees and pray for God's mercy to open our eyes to what love is.

If we see God's love more and more clearly, then our love for him will increase and we will be able to say with the psalmist, 'Whom have I in heaven but you? And earth has nothing I desire besides you' (Psalm 73:25). A child may live a totally self-centred life when young, taking their parents' care for granted, but then come to love and appreciate their parents more as they get older and realise the many sacrifices that they have made for their sake. In the same way, as we grow in our understanding of God's love for us and how much he cares about us, our love for him will also grow, and with it our desire to serve him.[67] As we serve him in love, we will be building our reward.

Love suffers

Love is always costly. If you love a poor person it will cost you money; if you love a lonely person it will cost you time to be with them; if you love a distressed person it will cost you emotional energy and a shoulder to cry on.

---

[67] John 14:21, 23.

What does it mean to show love for God, if not to suffer and go through all kinds of difficulties and troubles for his sake? 1 John 3:16 reminds us, 'This is how we know what love is: Jesus Christ laid down his life for us. And we ought to lay down our lives for our brothers and sisters.' Love is not primarily about words and feelings but action, and God demonstrated his love for us in the cross. God has always been concerned that if we claim to love him then we will love those around us, as Jesus reminded Peter three times when he met him after the resurrection.[68]

God will never need anything from us, never be hungry or thirsty, never be depressed, sick or lonely, but people around us will be. We cannot meet any need of God to show him love, but he takes whatever we do for the least of his creatures personally as if we did it for him,[69] just as any loving father would take it as helping him if someone helped one of his children in want or danger. So it is that helping the least, most insignificant person is equivalent in God's sight to helping Jesus himself.

We have already explored how knowing God is the greatest possible treasure, and Paul writes in Philippians 3:10, 'I want to know Christ and the power of his resurrection and the fellowship of sharing in his sufferings, becoming like him in his death' (NIV 1984). Very often it is only the first part of this verse that is quoted: 'I want to know Christ and the power of his resurrection' – which sounds very encouraging. We all

---

[68] John 21:15–17.

[69] Matthew 25:31–46.

want to experience the power of Jesus' resurrection in our lives, but what about 'the fellowship of sharing in his sufferings, becoming like him in his death'? What does that mean and how does it help us to know God?

In the film *The Hurt Locker*, we are introduced to an American army team of bomb disposal experts working in the war in Iraq. The tension builds as one of them tries to defuse a bomb not knowing whether he will succeed or be blown to pieces any minute. The others are frantically urging him on and there is huge relief when he manages to neutralise the explosive. The next day, however, they are back doing the same thing, and so on day after day. On one occasion, a man pleads with them to rescue him from a suicide bomb vest but they fail and he is blown up in front of them. We see them roughhousing in horseplay in the evenings, releasing the pent-up anxiety and tension.

Later, one of them goes home to America on leave. He goes back to everyday suburban life, shopping in the supermarket with his wife and playing with his kids, but it is a different world to his life in Iraq. It soon becomes clear that his wife cannot really understand what he has gone through and so no longer knows the man he has become. His fellow soldiers back in Iraq are the ones who really know him because they have been through the same experience and understand what that feels like and what effect it has on a person.

If we really want to know Christ, we need to learn to see the world as he sees it and to love as he loves – to find out what real love is. This is not through intellectual knowledge but in real experience. It is one thing to know something in our heads; it is quite another to actually experience it. You can read all you like about falling in love, marriage, childbirth, bringing up children or losing a loved one, but it is only those who have experienced these things that really know what they mean. If we are ever going to know Christ and his love, we need to be willing to love and suffer as he did, and indeed share in the fellowship of his sufferings in order to understand him and become like him.

Suffering because of love then becomes our friend and we can say with Paul, 'we also glory in our sufferings, because we know that suffering produces perseverance; perseverance, character; and character, hope' (Romans 5:3–4). If our love persists through suffering then it has grown stronger and the perseverance has led to growth in our spiritual character and likeness to Christ. Jesus also commends such suffering in his cause and says that it has rich reward in heaven: 'Blessed are you when people insult you, persecute you and falsely say all kinds of evil against you because of me. Rejoice and be glad, because great is your reward in heaven' (Matthew 5:11–12).

The greatest love (and therefore what merits the greatest reward) is shown by the greatest suffering, and Jesus declares, 'Greater love has no one than this: to lay down one's life for one's friends' (John 15:13). Because Jesus suffered more in his love for God the Father and for us than anyone else, he has the highest honour in heaven. Paul writes that Jesus, 'being in very nature God, did not consider equality with God something to be used to his own advantage; rather, he made himself nothing by taking the very nature of a servant, being made in human likeness. And being found in appearance as a man, he humbled himself by becoming obedient to death – even death on a cross! Therefore God exalted him to the highest place and gave him the name that is above every name' (Philippians 2:6–9). Jesus went from the highest of heights, being eternally God himself, to take the lowest, most awful place, identifying with the sin of the world and becoming sin for us because he loved God the Father and wanted to do his will and because he loved us and wanted to save us. There could be no greater love, and so he has the highest place in heaven.

If we want to share that inheritance then we have to share his mindset[70] and share in his sufferings: 'Now if we are children, then we are heirs – heirs of God and co-heirs with Christ, if indeed we share in his sufferings in order that we may also share in his glory' (Romans 8:17–18). We have to learn what real love is and to love as Jesus did, becoming like him in actually experiencing dying to ourselves (not necessarily physically dying for our faith, of course) and finding joy in serving others. This does not mean that we go out looking for suffering or inflicting it on ourselves, whipping ourselves like some mediaeval monks did. We do not need to go looking for it, as real love for God and others will always involve suffering at some point, probably sooner rather than later!

Imagine being told that for 30 seconds before we were born, we could undergo some kind of uncomfortable test or trial and the result would determine how we lived for the whole of our life on earth – whether we were really successful, average, or disadvantaged in some way.

---

70 Philippians 2:5.

Would you think that you could not be bothered about striving to do well in the test, or would you try as hard as you could because your whole future depended on it? Well, the reality is much more dramatic than that – what we do in this life of 70 or 80 years or so determines our destiny forever! After a million years, we will not even have made a dent in eternity.

Will we not pour all our energy and enthusiasm into serving God by faith in his power at work within us now? In 2 Corinthians 4:17 Paul says, 'For our light and momentary troubles are achieving for us an eternal glory that far outweighs them all.' Later in that letter, Paul tells us that his 'light and momentary troubles' involved constant danger and hardship, often going without food, receiving 39 lashes five times, being beaten with rods, being stoned and being shipwrecked. Yet he did not care because the eyes of his faith were fixed on the eternal reward being stored up for him.

Let us examine our Christian lives. What have we done for God? Sadhu Sundar Singh reportedly said, 'We have but this one life in which to bear the cross for Christ.' May God save us from missing the chance because of the love of an easy life.

But how does this love translate into treasure in heaven?

9
Currency of Love

What is heaven like? This is a question that so many of us must have wondered about without drawing any real conclusions. There is always the classic picture of people lounging around on clouds playing harps and being served by angels, but that, of course, is just a popular cliché, and not very inspiring or exciting either! In his writings, C. S. Lewis pictured heaven as a land that is more real than this world, with beckoning uplands where there are always more joyful wonders to explore.

My grandmother once asked me what I thought heaven would be like (she lived to be 103), as she had a very simple and uninformed Roman Catholic faith. I said to her, 'Well, you go to church to be near to God and so maybe it is like a very long church service that lasts forever.'

She was very shocked and quickly said, 'I certainly hope not!' as she had always found such services boring. I tried to encourage her by saying that maybe that type of service did not reflect what it was really like to be near God.

Of course, we cannot imagine the details of what heaven will be like, as the Bible tells us in 1 Corinthians 2:9, 'No eye has seen, no ear has heard, no mind has conceived what God has prepared for those who love him' (NIV 1984). The human mind can actually only imagine things it has already experienced, which is why science fiction aliens are always like human beings or some other earthly life form, and why we are always surprised by new discoveries in the universe. Think of a colour you have never seen. Got it? Of course not – you can't do it! We can only think of variations of colours that we know. Although there are colours beyond the human visible spectrum (bees can see ultraviolet), we cannot imagine them. If we are unable to do such a simple thing, then how could we ever imagine reality outside this physical universe!

The Bible does tell us, however, that God is going to make all things new by creating new heavens and a new earth, without evil, pain, disease or death.[71] I am sure that all the variety and beauty of this creation will be reflected in and exceeded by the new one. It will be a place of perfect love, joy and peace and the key element will be that any barrier between God and humanity will be gone and God will dwell with his people. 'God's dwelling-place is now among the people, and he will dwell with them. They will be his people, and God himself will be with them and be their God. "He will wipe every tear from their eyes. There will be no more death" or mourning or crying or pain, for the old order of things has passed away' (Revelation 21:3–4).

These verses talk about the end of all suffering and pain, and in fact we are told that we will not even

---

[71] Isaiah 65:17–25; Revelation 21:1–5.

remember such things – or indeed this whole world: 'See, I will create new heavens and a new earth. The former things will not be remembered, nor will they come to mind' (Isaiah 65:17). It seems that only faith, hope and love will remain past that barrier.[72] If, then, we will not even remember worldly things, how much more should we focus on the eternal value of God's love and make it our aim to grow in that towards God and those around us?[73] Anything else that we use our energy and resources to build for ourselves in this world will pass away and ultimately be forgotten. It is the relationships built in God's love that will last into the new creation; the natural relationships of this world are temporary – even those as close as marriage[74] (in the sense that one would remain a husband or wife forever).

Because our minds cannot grasp it, God uses pictures to describe what we will be like in the next world. One such picture is found in 1 Corinthians 15:35–38. Here, our present bodies are likened to seeds which are sown into the ground to 'die' and be used up to produce a plant. Imagine that you had only ever seen seeds: small dried-up things of different shapes, sizes and colours. If that was all you had ever seen, you could not possibly imagine that such things could produce the beauty of a flower or a tree, let alone think what a whole garden or forest would look like. What a wonderful picture of our future state with God, which is going to be so much more beautiful and wonderful than we could ever conceive

---

[72] 1 Corinthians 13:8–13.

[73] 2 Corinthians 4:18; 2 Peter 3:11–13.

[74] Matthew 22:30.

now and as marvellously unimaginable as a flowering shrub growing from a shrivelled-up seed!

Another description of heaven is as the marriage feast of the Lamb (that is, Jesus). Now marriage feasts are not boring; they are times of good food, dancing and rejoicing that a long-anticipated love is about to be fulfilled. Someone once asked me, 'In heaven, do we just stand about looking at God?' That does not describe a marriage feast!

In fact, the Bible says that God instituted marriage, the most intimate and lifelong human relationship, as a picture of the love he wants to share with each of us.[75] The Church is described as the bride of Christ, and doesn't every bride want to look her best for her husband on their wedding day? I have conducted many weddings, and that is surely the day when every woman shines brightest. Our 'wedding day' is when we arrive in heaven and are presented to Jesus. We are made beautiful in his sight by the deeds we have done in the power of his Spirit – acts of his love and kindness.[76] How are we going to look?

Love is its own reward

What is treasure in heaven? It is, as we have already seen, primarily to know and love God, who is perfect love himself. We are made in the image of our Creator God of love and it is love which fulfils the human heart. Without it, life has no worthwhile meaning, and with it, a human

---

[75] Ephesians 5:31–32.
[76] Revelation 19:7–8.

being can endure the most awful trials and rise to the highest joys. As a creature to our Creator and as a saved and forgiven sinner to our Saviour, that love is expressed as wholehearted worship and thankfulness for his love for us.

The picture of heaven we find in the book of Revelation is one of continual worship of God for his goodness in creation and for Jesus dying to save us.[77] In fact, the worship ratchets up from being spoken to being sung as it focuses on the ultimate demonstration of God's love for us in Jesus' sacrifice. To realise fully in heaven what we only dimly understand now – the sheer extent of God's love for us in Christ – will bring an ecstatic flood of joy. God's first and most important command to us, to love him with all our heart, soul and mind,[78] is actually what fulfils us as creatures, and he is telling us to do it for our own good!

If you love someone, it is a joy to do something to please them, and the joy of pleasing a parent, friend, child, wife or husband is just a faint reflection of the joy of heaven. The more we love God, the greater will be the reward of joy in pleasing our beloved Father and doing something for the Saviour who gave everything to rescue us from eternal death. The more we realise how much he has loved us and all he has done for us, then the more exquisite, the more overwhelming, will be the joy when we think that we, who were once lost and without hope in selfishness, sin and despair, could have pleased him by his grace, and when we hear the words, 'Well done, my

---

[77] Revelation 4:6 – 5:14.

[78] Matthew 22:37–38.

good and faithful servant' (Matthew 25:23, NLT). Because of this, even the smallest act of love will bring its own reward.

The reverse is also true that any religious act we might do in this world has no reward in heaven if it is done out of pride, duty or ritual, without love. Jesus said, 'When you pray, do not be like the hypocrites, for they love to pray standing in the synagogues and on the street corners to be seen by others. Truly I tell you, they have received their reward in full' (Matthew 6:5). If our motive for doing something, even as 'religious' as praying, prophesying or spreading the gospel, is to get the acclaim of others and not out of express love for God, then that acclaim is the only reward we will get. Of course, no one prays on street corners to be seen these days – but what about posting on Facebook?

As human beings we can be impressed by supernatural power and miracles, by great Bible knowledge, insight, wisdom and gifts of preaching, and by extreme commitment to God's cause, even martyrdom, but none of it means anything to God without love. Let us remind ourselves of some of the most famous verses in the Bible, often read out at weddings because of their emphasis on love: 'If I speak in the tongues of men or of angels, but do not have love, I am only a resounding gong or a clanging cymbal. If I have the gift of prophecy and can fathom all mysteries and all knowledge, and if I have a faith that can move mountains, but do not have love, I am nothing. If I give all I possess to the poor and give over my body to hardship that I may boast, but do not have love, I gain nothing' (1 Corinthians 13:1–3).

This could not be clearer, that the only thing that is rewarded in heaven is love and that anything else we might do is worth absolutely nothing in God's sight, no matter how impressive it might seem on earth.

Love for others

Just as love for God is rewarded in heaven, so is love for those around us. Jesus linked the command to love our neighbour as much as we love ourselves with the first and greatest command to love God.[79] Again this is for our own good, as our joy in this life and the next will grow as we love and serve others. There is an old Christian cliché that JOY means Jesus first, Others second and Yourself last, and there is a lot of truth in that. Jesus said, 'Give, and it will be given to you. A good measure, pressed down, shaken together and running over, will be poured into your lap. For with the measure you use, it will be measured to you' (Luke 6:38).

When we love someone, then it is not a problem but rather a joy to serve them. Paradoxically, the greater the effort or pain to help them, the greater the joy when we see the result of our efforts in blessing them – think of the joy of a mother when a child is born after the pain of giving birth, or think of a parent's joy at their son or daughter's graduation after all they have done to bring them up and help them study.

Paul referred to the believers at Thessalonica and Philippi (and elsewhere), whom he had seen come to

[79] Matthew 22:39.

99

salvation in Jesus and had built up in their faith by his teaching and counselling, as his 'joy and crown' whom he loved and in whom he would glory in heaven.[80] Because he loved them so much, it would be fantastic for him to see them in heaven, to see what beautiful grace and glory God had built into them and to think that he had been used to help bring that about. Of course, he would only feel that joy if he really loved them; anything done simply out of duty (as a state employee might deal with a benefits client) would leave him indifferent to the outcome. Again, love produces its own reward.

A highlight of my whole life was a trip to one of the slums in Lusaka, Zambia. I had done missionary training in India and it always bothered me that we had no money to help with the extreme poverty that I saw around me (in fact, the team that I was with often had barely enough money to eat). When I returned to the UK from India, I set up a charity shop to sell goods from the developing world and help the poor that way, but I never saw the result of any help we gave or any money we collected to help specific disasters.

When I went with a team to Zambia, however, we held a children's club for local slum kids. We had brought coloured pens and paper with us to give them and they were so excited to receive such simple gifts. About 100 children aged from 2 to 18 came along each day. The young men with me asked them to copy down one of the Ten Commandments, only for us to realise that they could

---

[80] Philippians 4:1; 1 Thessalonians 2:19–20.

not write (the guys w
first local school to be bu

I sat with the grannies wh
as many of their parents had die
realised that they too were so thrill
coloured felt-tip pens. They were happ
colours they each had. One of them was t
the simple sentence that was to be copied do
became clear that they too would have difficulty w
could just about hold back the tears as I slowly w
capital letters for one of them to copy. It was such a joy to
be able to do something to help and to see the result of
our efforts in the foundations of the school taking shape.
In many ways a simple thing, but it meant so much.

Imagine we send some money overseas to help in a
famine or natural disaster and we never see what result
that had. But when we arrive in heaven, we are
approached by people who say, 'You are the ones who
gave, and because of you, my family lived and here they
are.' What an amazing joy! No wonder Jesus talked about
making friends in heaven.[81]

If the currency of heaven is love, how is your account
doing?

---

[81] Luke 16:9.

bout positions of
y I tell you, at the
of Man sits on his
red me will also sit
tribes of Israel. And
everyone who has rothers or sisters or
father or mother or wife or child or fields for my sake
will receive a hundred times as much and will inherit
eternal life. But many who are first will be last, and many
who are last will be first' (Matthew 19:28–30). We find the
risen Lord saying the same thing in Revelation 2:26: 'To
the one who is victorious and does my will to the end, I
will give authority over the nations.'

There is also the implication that how we steward the
things God gives us in this life will determine how much
he trusts us to look after in the next: 'If you have not been
trustworthy in handling worldly wealth, who will trust
you with true riches? And if you have not been
trustworthy with someone else's property, who will give
you property of your own?' (Luke 16:11–12). Everything
we have in this life is ultimately dust and ashes as it is
temporary and so does not really belong to us. If we
cannot handle that properly, then why would we do any

better with things of eternal value that would be ours forever?

Indeed, when the disciples realised this, they began quarrelling amongst themselves about who would be greatest in the future kingdom of heaven, which they imagined would be an earthly empire like that of King David. Shortly after Jesus talked about thrones in heaven, the mother of James and John (who were probably only in their twenties at the time) came to him to ask if they could be his right- and left-hand men when he formed his government.[82] Jesus told them that they did not know what they were asking because authority in his kingdom is linked to 'drinking from his cup', referring to the sacrifice of the cross. As we have already seen, it is the greater love that is more rewarded in heaven. He also said that those places at his right and left belonged to those for whom they had been prepared by God the Father.

When further argument broke out amongst the other ten apostles, Jesus called them together to teach them that authority in his kingdom comes from humbling oneself to become a servant, even a slave, to others, 'just as the Son of Man did not come to be served, but to serve, and to give his life as a ransom for many' (Matthew 20:28). It is the self-effacing, humble service of love in laying down one's life (time, energy, resources, ambitions and dreams) for others that lifts a person up in the kingdom of God.

---

[82] Matthew 20:20–28.

The way up is down

It is a great paradox that the way to gain the treasure of eternal life is to lose our life by laying down our priorities in order to serve others. If we seek to gain life here by serving our selfish motives, we lose out on the real treasure of knowing God's love.[83]

Love is not proud or self-seeking because it is concerned about the loved one and not itself. Pride, which is concerned about its own honour and position and not about others, is the complete opposite to love, and incompatible with it. Pride will lead to envy, arrogance and selfish ambition, and will often result in despising those who are weaker and hating those who are stronger. It is the source of so much division and conflict. Love, however, is so taken up with the loved one that it forgets itself and becomes truly humble.

Jesus gave advice about a guest attending a wedding feast.[84] He said that when you go to sit down, do not sit near the high table as someone may ask you to move lower down as the seat was reserved for a closer friend or family member. You would then end up being humiliated in front of everyone else. Rather take a very low place and then the host will invite you to move up higher. Jesus concluded by saying that all those who put themselves higher will be brought down (by God) and all those who humble themselves will be lifted up.

The Bible says, 'God opposes the proud but shows favour to the humble' (1 Peter 5:5). Pride is actually a lie

---

[83] Luke 9:24.

[84] Luke 14:7–11.

104

as all good things come from God, and he should be given the praise and honour for them. The Bible points out that every good thing we have, we received as a gift from God,[85] including, of course, all our physical attributes, intelligence, skills and creativity. If, then, all these things are gifts that we have been given, how can we be proud of them? My father is an artist and has given me a really great picture of a tiger cub which hangs in my lounge. When people admire that painting, if I were to say, 'Do you like what I have done in this picture?', I would simply be lying and taking the praise for it for myself rather than giving it where it belongs. Similarly, we are lying if we are proud of our intelligence, abilities, good looks, etc. when all these things are gifts of God. God actively opposes the proud in order to frustrate selfish ambitions, and some of the torment of hell will be the rage of thwarted and helpless pride.

Mary prophesied about what God would do through the holy child that would be born to her: 'he has scattered those who are proud in their inmost thoughts. He has brought down rulers from their thrones but has lifted up the humble' (Luke 1:51–52), as did Simeon when he met Mary and Joseph with the baby Jesus in the temple courts: 'This child is destined to cause the falling and rising of many in Israel' (Luke 2:34).

Jesus modelled God's kind of leadership authority by having no palaces, leading no armies and spending years trudging the lanes of Israel with few possessions and often nowhere to sleep at night. Day after day, he

---

[85] 1 Corinthians 4:7.

faithfully healed and taught the people even when he and his disciples were tired and exhausted, and he patiently bore the mistrust, lies and abuse of the authorities. Although he had all the support of the crowds, and his supernatural power, he did not threaten or retaliate. He did not stand on his honour as the Messiah, the Son of God, but humbly bore insults and contempt. He taught his disciples that whoever humbles themselves like a little child is the greatest in the kingdom of heaven.[86]

Finally, when he knew he would be tortured to death the next day, he got down on his hands and knees and washed his disciples' feet, taking the place of the lowest servant, to their great embarrassment and confusion. How could God's chosen King be found on the floor washing his followers' feet? He said he did it as an example that they should follow.[87]

Lifting up the humble

We have already seen that the values of God's kingdom do not reflect the values of this world that honour intelligence, talent, riches and power. God is concerned about love and kindness, self-sacrifice and humility. This means that he values every act of kindness, no matter how small or seemingly insignificant: 'if anyone gives even a cup of cold water to one of these little ones who is my disciple, truly I tell you, that person will certainly not lose their reward' (Matthew 10:42).

---

[86] Matthew 18:4.
[87] John 13:1–17.

It is not necessarily the famous figures who do great public things for God who will be most honoured in his kingdom, although they will surely receive a reward for what they do. Human beings see only the way things appear outwardly, but God looks on the heart,[88] and he will reward according to the love and devotion of the heart. This is so wonderful because it means that all the millions of ordinary people are not at a disadvantage to the talented few when it comes to rewards in God's kingdom.

We see this very clearly when Jesus commented on those giving gifts to the temple treasury. Rich people came and gave maybe the equivalent of thousands of pounds, sometimes with a servant going before them to announce their gift with a trumpet![89] They would be seen and respected by the crowds. But then a poor widow came and put in two very small copper coins. These coins would make practically no difference to the temple treasury's total funds and she came and went entirely unnoticed. Jesus, however, was watching, and he said that she gave more than all the others because they gave what they could easily afford out of their wealth whilst she 'put in all she had to live on'.[90]

The widow was unseen by the rest of the world, but not by God. He saw the devotion of her heart and commended her, and God is searching the hearts of all humankind. His kingdom is not primarily about efficiency and the success of huge results (good as those

---

[88] 1 Samuel 16:7.

[89] Matthew 6:2.

[90] Luke 21:1–4.

may be), but about wholehearted love and sold-out devotion. It means that the simple kindness of the weak and powerless is at least as valuable to God as the offerings of the rich and talented, if it cost them more to do it.

A dramatic early twentieth-century example is that of a poor African woman who found the joy of forgiveness of sins and a new life through faith in Christ. Others were coming, bringing their offerings to the altar, but she was so poor that she had nothing to give. She so desperately wanted to give something back to the Lord who had loved her so much as to die in her place that she went and sold herself to a plantation owner as a slave for life and brought the silver dollar she earned as an offering!

For someone struggling with physical or emotional pain, to offer simple hospitality may cost them more, and so mean more to God, than someone from a privileged and well-balanced Christian background spending some time on a mission trip. We are not to judge, of course, and only God can see the heart, but thank God that no act of mercy and kindness done in the power of his Spirit will go unnoticed, and one day he will judge absolutely justly, and all the unfairness of this world will be undone. He has told us that when we get to heaven there will be many surprises. Many who are famous and prominent in this world will be last, and many who are completely unknown now will be first.

The godly ambition to be great in the kingdom of heaven is good, but are we willing to allow ourselves to go low enough to achieve it?

11
Where the Heart Is

You can always tell where someone's treasure is. In conversation they may show polite interest in whatever is being discussed, but if it goes on too long then you may notice them getting distracted and their eyes glazing over. Their mobile phone suddenly becomes more interesting and pressing. I'm sure we have all experienced that, from both sides! But if you hit on a topic they treasure, be it football, fast cars, babies, the latest fashion, making money, their holidays or career achievements, then they quickly come alive, their eyes light up and their conversation becomes animated and fully engaged. It is an interesting observation on human nature that in small talk, most people love to talk about themselves, and many will happily do so for hours! Jesus said, 'where your treasure is, there your heart will be also' (Matthew 6:21).

When I was a fairly new Christian, a friend and I were praying for one of our fellow students to find salvation in Jesus. On hearing the news that he had put his faith in the Lord and wanted to follow him, we literally danced for joy around the college quad. Youthful exuberance, but filled with joy because the treasure of another precious life had been saved.

What gets us excited? Is it the idea of coming into a lot of money, some new promotion at work, or meeting a new love interest? Or is it walking through life with the living God, being filled with his love and helping others to find the same blessing in their lives?

Guard your heart

When we talk about the human heart, we are not talking about the organ that pumps blood around the body, but the innermost person, the source of our deepest motivation that energises our life. The Bible warns us that the condition of our heart should be our top priority in life: 'Above all else, guard your heart, for everything you do flows from it' (Proverbs 4:23).

In common language, if we haven't the heart for the fight, we give up; if we haven't the heart to tell someone something, we keep quiet; if we haven't the heart to continue a relationship, we lose it. How much heart do we have for the things of God, and how can we remedy a loss of heart for him? How can we guard our heart?

The key is to be found in what Jesus said in Matthew 6:21, that our heart will be wherever our treasure is. That is why the whole concept of treasure in heaven and understanding what God has to say about it is so important in maintaining and growing in the Christian life. We need to have our eyes fixed on the hope we have waiting for us in heaven.

But in the comfortable society of the developed world, it can almost be taboo to think about death, and life after death. The good life is for living now, and death is something to be put at the back of your mind, and to be dealt with by subconscious denial. Increasing lifespans and material comfort and health mean that all our emphasis is on the life we have in this world. This contrasts markedly with the ever-lurking threat of death in previous centuries and less fortunate parts of our present world. What is wrong with that? Isn't increasing health and longevity a good thing, and surely we should say good riddance to poverty and deprivation? On one level, of course, yes.

If this mentality dominates in the Church, however, it can lead to a 'gospel' that emphasises this present life. At its worst this becomes, 'Come to Jesus and he will make you healthy, wealthy and successful.' Of course, God is not a God of sickness, poverty and failure, and he does heal and bless, but we also find, 'Better the little that the righteous have than the wealth of many wicked' (Psalm 37:16), and, 'woe to you who are rich, for you have already received your comfort' (Luke 6:24). Why do the righteous normally have little? Because it is the ruthless and selfish who have usually dominated the earth and the righteous have given away all of their excess wealth to help those in severe poverty to survive.

Calling for people to return to godly living, John the Baptist came preaching, 'Anyone who has two shirts should share with the one who has none, and anyone who has food should do the same' (Luke 3:11). This is very basic and would leave each person involved with only one shirt to wear. The righteous would have little indeed! Jesus said, 'Do to others as you would have them do to you' (Luke 6:31).

111

Imagine you have swapped places with a family living on the street in India or Africa; that family is now here with all your goods and you and your family are in their dire circumstances with very little to eat and no education for your children. What would you want them to do to help you? Well, you probably would not want them to go hungry or lose their place to live or the things they need to do their work and survive, but you would want them to think before they spent money on luxuries they did not really need so that they could send any spare money for your family to at least get by. 'If anyone has material possessions and sees a brother or sister in need but has no pity on them, how can the love of God be in that person?' (1 John 3:17).

At the very least, an emphasis on this life leads to a 'gospel' of self-fulfilment and ease: 'Come to Jesus and he will give you a peaceful and fulfilled life.' Many sermons talk about how to find ways to serve God that 'fulfil who you are'. Whilst the fulfilment that comes from using the gifts God has given is good and great, how many people are going to feel fulfilled washing filthy feet or being nailed to a cross?

The idea of self-sacrifice is lost, and people are promised a rose-coloured Christian life where all their problems will be solved and troubles will be avoided by God's intervention. Yet Jesus said, 'I have told you these things, so that in me you may have peace. In this world you will have trouble. But take heart! I have overcome the world' (John 16:33), and Paul says, 'If only for this life we have hope in Christ, we are of all people most to be pitied' (1 Corinthians 15:19). Someone has said, 'If your gospel is "Come to Jesus for health, wealth and happiness", then people will think you worship health, wealth and happiness, not Jesus.'

No, the gospel message is to turn away from living the world's way and to trust in Jesus for forgiveness and the gift of a relationship with God, which is eternal life. Our hope is not in this world but in the next: 'So we fix our eyes not on what is seen, but on what is unseen, since what is seen is temporary, but what is unseen is eternal' (2 Corinthians 4:18). It is so important, then, that our Christian hope is set, and the eyes of our faith are fixed, not on the things of this world which will pass away, but on the glory and treasure waiting for us in heaven, for where our treasure is, that is where our heart will be also.[91]

Motivation for living

It is clear that without the concept of inheritance, reward or treasure in heaven, a major motivation in the Christian life is absent. People sometimes think that such a motive would be too self-interested, but Jesus was not beyond appealing to our self-interest in his teaching.

In Luke's Gospel there is a rather strange parable about a dishonest manager. On hearing that he is about to lose his job because of his mismanagement, he calls in each of his master's debtors and reduces how much they owe. He thinks that by doing these corrupt favours, he will make friends for himself when he is put out of

---

[91] Matthew 6:21.

work.[92] Jesus seems to commend the self-interest and crafty behaviour of this plainly dishonest man, but what point is he really making?

At the end of the parable Jesus declares, 'You cannot serve both God and money' (Luke 16:13), and so it is clear that he is not talking about money. He is talking about treasure in heaven: 'I tell you, use worldly wealth to gain friends for yourselves, so that when it is gone, you will be welcomed into eternal dwellings' (Luke 16:9). Jesus is saying that it is better to use things that you know you are going to lose (like the dishonest manager knew he was going to lose his job and opportunity to do favours for his master's debtors), such as worldly wealth, by giving them away to the poor who will then welcome you with joy into heaven.

In fact, we are told in the Bible that we cannot please God unless we trust in his rewards. Hebrews 11:6 says, 'without faith it is impossible to please God, because anyone who comes to him must believe that he exists and that he rewards those who earnestly seek him'. Such faith is a vital motivation in wanting to seek God. It is an insult to God to think that he is not worth seeking.

It is a great paradox, however, that the rewards God holds out for us are to be gained through selfless love and not selfish motives. It is necessary to put to death our selfish motives and to lay down our life's dreams and ambitions (which God may give back to us with a new motivation to serve him, or show us better ones) in order to gain the real treasure of God's love in Jesus. As he

92 Luke 16:1–12.

himself said, 'Whoever wants to be my disciple must deny themselves and take up their cross and follow me. For whoever wants to save their life will lose it, but whoever loses their life for me will find it' (Matthew 16:24–25). It is God's wonderful, glorious, selfless love that is the aim, the motivation and the reward for our Christian service.

When life gets difficult and the going gets tough, we can falter in our commitment to serving God and doing the right thing. The sheer persistence of problems or years of fighting the same battles may cause us to grow tired and weary in our walk with God. In such circumstances, we can be tempted to give up or become lazy and sit out the Christian life on the sidelines of the race others are running. We need to join ourselves up to Jesus afresh and let him give us strength,[93] and find the motivation to carry on by setting our sights on the hope that is laid out before us, as Jesus fixed his eyes on the joy of the Father's love and winning our souls to endure the cross.[94] 'Let us not become weary in doing good, for at the proper time we will reap a harvest if we do not give up' (Galatians 6:9).

What motivates your Christian walk?

---

[93] Matthew 11:28–30.

[94] Hebrews 12:2.

12

What is Our Response?

Faced with such a great salvation, with God who destined us in love to be his children before the creation of the world, who came in Jesus to pay the price to win us back when we were lost and separated from him in disobedience and sin, and who has planned to transform us into his glorious image once again and crown us with glory with him forever, what should be our response? Can you see the treasure hidden in the field? What are you going to do to get it?

How we respond to God's invitation in all this will determine our destiny forever. Will we arrive in heaven to hear, 'Well done, good and faithful servant',[95] or will we enter 'as one escaping through the flames' of the destruction of a basically selfish life?[96] Are we growing in understanding God's love for us, or has our Christian life become a matter of cold and distant routine? Can we say with the psalmist that one day in God's presence is better than a thousand elsewhere?[97]

---

[95] Matthew 25:21, 23.

[96] 1 Corinthians 3:15.

[97] Psalm 84:10.

Set your hope

Talking about the temporary nature of this world, that all our knowledge and prophecies will pass away, Paul says that three things will remain: faith, hope and love.[98] Faith is the means by which we enter into and live in a relationship with God, and love is the aim, but the middle word, hope, is often neglected. Yet it is emphasised so much in New Testament teaching: 'For everything that was written in the past was written to teach us, so that through the endurance taught in the Scriptures and the encouragement they provide we might have hope' (Romans 15:4); 'we ourselves, who have the firstfruits of the Spirit, groan inwardly as we wait eagerly for our adoption to sonship, the redemption of our bodies. For in this hope we were saved' (Romans 8:23–24); 'with minds that are alert and fully sober, set your hope on the grace to be brought to you when Jesus Christ is revealed at his coming' (1 Peter 1:13).

These verses tell us that the Scriptures were written to give us hope. We were saved in hope of a future eternal life and we are commanded to fix our minds on that hope. Now we use the word 'hope' in different ways. We say, 'We hope it will be a nice day tomorrow,' meaning that we would like it to be a nice day but we are not sure it will be. This is not the meaning of the Greek word *elpis*, translated 'hope' in the Bible, which actually means 'a confident expectation'. This is more like saying, 'We are working hard in the hope of a good result,' meaning that we are expecting a good result because of our hard work.

---

[98] 1 Corinthians 13:8–13.

The Bible encourages us to look beyond the troubles of this life in confident expectation of being made anew in a redeemed universe of new heavens and new earth, without sin, pain, sorrow, disease or death, in perfect love, joy and peace with the God who has loved us so much forever. As Christians, forgiven and brought from death to eternal life, we should be looking forward to the life beyond death. If we are not, it is because we have not fully understood or accepted the message of the New Testament about the glories that await us. At the end of the book of Revelation, after Jesus has said that he is coming back soon, the response rings out, 'The Spirit and the bride say, "Come!" And let the one who hears say, "Come!"' (Revelation 22:17).

Years ago when I was running our charity shop, we used to have many conversations about spiritual things with the atheist hairdresser from the shop next door. We had a very godly elderly volunteer in his seventies, and one day this hairdresser confessed to him that he was afraid of death. The old man said, 'Oh, I don't know, I'm quite looking forward to it.' For days afterwards, the hairdresser could not stop talking about it!

Imagine you have been promised an all-expenses-paid world cruise. As the time approaches for your holiday, you are looking forward to all that you are going to see and to just taking it easy and relaxing. The prospect of such a wonderful adventure makes all the other troubles you are facing that much more bearable, because you are thinking that it is not much longer before you can relax on your cruise. Heaven is infinitely better than a world cruise! If we are not looking forward to it but are clinging on to this world, then maybe we need to examine our hearts as to how much we actually believe in it.

When we do set our hope on the prospect of a life filled with perfect love and joy with our beloved God and Saviour in heaven, it lifts our hearts in the here and now, and we feel the first stirrings of heavenly joy. With that hope within us, we are strengthened against all the trials and temptations that this world throws at us, and can persevere in everything God calls us to do.

Run the race to win the prize

If we truly see the treasure in the field and grasp the wonder and enormity of what God has done for us in Jesus, giving us the opportunity to be transformed into his image and to share his very life, then we will be eager to give up all other priorities and pour all our energy into following him and acquiring that treasure.

Paul talks about a race being laid out ahead for us to run. God planned out our lives in love long before we were born with a desire to glorify us and give us overflowing joy in the riches of his goodness.[99] 'For we are God's handiwork, created in Christ Jesus to do good works, which God prepared in advance for us to do' (Ephesians 2:10). We are all unique, and God has a unique plan for each one of us to make us like Jesus and heap us with blessings and treasure in heaven, which we will inherit by growing in acts of love and self-sacrifice carried

---

[99] Ephesians 1:3–12.

out in the power of his Spirit as we run the race he has set us.

If we grasp it, this is such an exciting thought, that God has laid out a spiritual adventure for each of us to bless us. It will be the hardest thing we ever do, but in the power of his Spirit, we will have his strength with which to accomplish it all, and he cannot fail! It was Paul's top priority in his God-given mission: 'I consider my life worth nothing to me; my only aim is to finish the race and complete the task the Lord Jesus has given me' (Acts 20:24), and, 'Do you not know that in a race all the runners run, but only one gets the prize? Run in such a way as to get the prize. Everyone who competes in the games goes into strict training. They do it to get a crown that will not last, but we do it to get a crown that will last for ever. Therefore I do not run like someone running aimlessly; I do not fight like a boxer beating the air' (1 Corinthians 9:24–26).

Athletes control everything they do in a strict training timetable. All the food they eat is monitored, as is their sleep and exercise time. They push themselves through the pain barrier in order to try to come first in their event, or break a world record. Even if they break that record, it will almost certainly not be long before someone else comes along and in turn breaks theirs; a lifetime's commitment and single-minded effort for a few weeks, months or maybe years of being in the limelight as the record holder. They do it all for the brief glory of being the number one in their sporting field, but we are looking forward to a prize and glory that will last for ever. How much more serious and committed should we be in pursuing our prize than an Olympic athlete?

The good news is that this race is not a competition with others but rather a personal challenge for ourselves.[100] Jesus gently rebuked his disciples when they started to argue about who would be greatest in his kingdom, and that way leads to all kinds of godless pride, envy and conflict. He told them that places in heaven have been allocated by God the Father, who already knows the whole course of each person's life from beginning to end. God had told this to the prophet Daniel centuries before: 'As for you, go your way till the end. You will rest, and then at the end of the days you will rise to receive your allotted inheritance' (Daniel 12:13). So we are not in a competitive race.

We cannot even adequately judge our own inward motives, let alone those of others, and so there is certainly no wisdom in endless introspection or casting judgements over other people. Comparing ourselves with others is most unwise, and the Lord's command is to humbly value others above ourselves.[101] The best we can do is to keep a clear conscience before the Lord, repenting and trusting him for the power to change whenever the Holy Spirit convicts us that we have gone wrong. Paul says this about himself: 'I do not even judge myself. My conscience is clear, but that does not make me innocent. It is the Lord who judges me. Therefore judge nothing before the appointed time; wait until the Lord comes. He will bring to light what is hidden in darkness and will expose the

---

[100] Galatians 6:4.

[101] Philippians 2:3.

motives of the heart. At that time each will receive their praise from God' (1 Corinthians 4:3–5).

I have quoted a lot from the writings of Paul in this book, as God has put him forward in the New Testament as the disciple of the risen Jesus whose life, teaching and heart we are told most about. In the letter to the Philippian Church, written towards the end of his life, he sums up what has been his priority as he has followed Jesus. He says that he considers all the rights, privileges and legalistic righteousness he had as one of the leaders of the Jewish faith as rubbish because knowing Jesus was worth so much more. He says that his overriding aim in life has been to know Jesus and the power of his resurrected life at work to change him and to share in his suffering love.[102]

As Paul sits for some years in a jail in Rome, not knowing whether or not he is about to be executed (he was eventually beheaded in the persecution that broke out under the emperor Nero), the vision of his faith is still set on the prize at the end of the race: 'I do not consider myself yet to have taken hold of it. But one thing I do: forgetting what is behind and straining towards what is ahead, I press on towards the goal to win the prize for which God has called me heavenwards in Christ Jesus' (Philippians 3:13–14).

Whether we have been following Jesus a few days, weeks or months, or for many years or decades, we can forget the past as God has dealt with all our failures on the cross, and we can leave him to judge the level of our

---

[102] Philippians 3:4–11.

faithfulness. We, like Paul, need to lift our eyes to that upward call of God in Jesus and to strain with all the energy and resources God gives us to win the treasure that he so wants us to have.

Can you see it, or is the treasure still hidden in the field? Are you ready to go and sell all that you have with joy to buy that field? No matter what it costs us, our wonderful God, the greatest treasure imaginable, is worth it.

'I pray that the eyes of your heart may be enlightened in order that you may know the hope to which he has called you, the riches of his glorious inheritance in his holy people, and his incomparably great power for us who believe' (Ephesians 1:18–19).